ENDORSEMENTS

Kim Maas

"We live in a moment in history when culture is rapidly transforming, nations are vying for power, and political opinions are fiercely dividing neighbors, friends and family. More than ever we need the voice of God. We need to know what He thinks, sees, feels, and wills for our lives, our families, our nations. Where do we begin? With the basics. Rachel Carroll, in her book, "The Voice of Love" has captured the heart of the Father as she lays the foundations for operating in the gift of prophecy. You will be equipped to begin to prophesy, and to build the prophetic culture on the inside so that you may participate in building the prophetic culture on the outside–in your church, city, region, and the nations. Rachel helps us begin the building process. This book is useful for individuals, training seminars, and small groups. Grab a friend and begin!"

Rev. Dr. Kim Maas
International Minister,
Founder/C.E.O Kim Maas Ministries

Author of Prophetic Community (Chosen Books: 2019), W: Wisdom, Wonder, Women, Facing Ziklag, and The Four Questions.

From Jamie Galloway

Rachel Carroll has wonderfully written a comprehensive must read on the prophetic in Voice of Love. Whether you are just discovering the voice of God or practicing advanced prophetic ministry this book will take your connection with the Spirit of Prophecy to the next level.

Jamie Galloway
Jamie Galloway Ministries
Prophetic Communicator
Author of Secrets of the Seer,
Hearing God's Voice & Supernatural Revolution.
jamiegalloway.com

Joy Weinzierl

Reading the 'Voice of Love' by Rachel Carroll is like opening a family heirloom chest filled with valuable treasure gained through a life marked by hunger, pursuit, and a daily walk with God. You too are invited to come close and learn what you were always created for..... to hear and walk closely with God who is the Voice of Love. As a New Testament prophet Rachel is gifted to equip you to hear God's voice and as a mother in the faith her passion is to see you thrive in your kingdom assignment as a son or daughter of God. The 'Voice of Love' will become a favorite resource for instruction and encouragement in your own pursuit of the Voice of Love.

Joy Weinzierl
Snr leader Grace Christian Church

Ivan Roman

My nickname early on in my ministry was the prophetic pit bull. When I was called into a meeting, people would tremble knowing I was about to tear them to shreds with my discernment. I wish I would have been given this book early in my prophetic journey. I would have learned just because what I was discerning was true didn't mean it was God revealing it to me. Gifts are given freely but the lens of our hearts can skewer Gods voice of love if we don't get healing.

Rachel does an incredible job of laying both a biblically balanced and passionate foundation built upon the goodness of God.
I found myself highlighting large portions of this book. Here's one quote I absolutely loved.

"Your belief about God and your value for Him form the foundation you'll build on. And those beliefs and values will determine how you prophesy. "

I have often said not to mistake and angry prophet for an angry God. Rachel takes her time and dissects the values that are needed in order to rightly represent the God of love.

I highly recommend Rachel Carrol as a friend of God and a prophet of love. Her ability to impart God's heart through the pages of this book will cause the reader to not only pursue a gift but the God of love Himself.

Ivan Roman
Ivan Roman
senior leader at Empowered Life Church

THE VOICE OF LOVE

Learning the Heart of Prophecy

Rachel Carroll

DEDICATION

We are who we are because of the broad shoulders of those who have poured into us. Those so beloved to the Lord, that only heaven knows all that they have done. I want to dedicate this book to Terry and Gerrie Hogg. You have always shown me what love looks like and what the voice of the Father sounds like. Always an open door, a warm fire and fresh scones in the oven! (the real Irish ones!) Wisdom and revelation are always close by and a balm for wounded hearts at the ready. I am forever grateful to know you as my dearest friends.

And of course Ian Carroll, the love of my life. You are one of the most strongest and most courageous people I know. Your passion for God is inspiring, and your deep love for the His church. You are always my biggest cheerleader, best friend, and the someone who has embodied generosity for as long as I have known you!

Thank you.

The Voice of Love
© 2019 Rachel Carroll

Building Contenders
Oak Park, Il, 60304 USA
rachel.carroll@greaterchicagochurch.com

ISBN: 978-0-9982644-4-8

TABLE OF CONTENTS

INTRODUCTION

Sometimes things are birthed out of necessity. Out of our own needs. Something we are looking for, but doesn't yet exist. Sometimes what you are looking for is something that you and only you can birth, because it's yours, it's part of your story that has yet to be written. Although you may not even know what will transpire from your journey, you do know that you have to do something and do it soon!

My love for the prophetic was birthed from a hunger to know God and hear his voice, it was a hunger that chased me down. This came at a time when I was looking for hope, encouragement and a place of "home." From this hunger a whole prophetic culture evolved. It grew and became so transformative, and continues to have wide reaching effects beyond anything I could ever have dreamed. The ripples of influence in all our lives are truly incredible. You can never tell or imagine for a second what difference one decision will make.

The cliché that huge oaks all started from tiny acorns is applicable right here. I really set out to find a way to survive, to find kindred spirits and re-establish a place of the presence of God. A place where I could rest and call my home. I was looking for a way to keep my head above water after my family and I moved from Northern Ireland to Chicago in June 2001.

This move to live in America for us as a family was monumental, possibly one of the biggest decisions I had ever made, only second to getting married.

I think of worship as a gathering place, like a huge fireplace that you pull up your chair, take off your shoes, and find yourself being able to take a deep breath. Letting everything settle, body, soul and spirit into this place of belonging. A remembering of who we are and where all the pieces begin to fit again. Many times we find there is a deep cry in us, an ache to be at rest and let all the "noise" stop, the agitation that is often an internal one. I believe this place is found in God Himself. His presence is so easily accessed through our worship and adoration, learning to never remove our gaze from His beautiful face.

I had always been involved in worship, in one shape or form, playing guitar, leading worship, loving the weaving of "The Song" with prayer that has always been home for me, it has always been the place I feel my best self, my truest, and most free.

Long before I came to America, I belonged to a gathering, a church, a people who were so hungry for God. A people who would sit, wait until the song arose from within the circle, then it would catch like a fire in all of us and just like very dry tinder the fire would begin. You could watch as the Holy Spirit moved around the room, each one given a different expression of worship.

I have had the privilege to sit at the feet of people who embodied the Father, who knew and loved Jesus in such a way that made me want him too, and who were such good friends with the Holy spirit, like I have rarely experienced. I had the honor of learning from them, and to watch as they effortlessly weaved in and out of worship with such grace and beauty. They made it look so easy, they were and continue to be true friends of the Holy Spirt. When we gathered, there was always a song to be sung, a prayer, a word of encouragement and a sense that Jesus is sitting right next to you, enjoying your friendship. When you have tasted of that beautiful presence, it is hard to be content with anything less.

Many years ago, a group of us went out to celebrate a friend's birthday. It was a special day and we ended up in a small fine dining establishment. There were around 7 courses and with each course the chef would come out and describe the dish. He had poured over these dishes and each course, better and better with incredible depths of flavors I had never experienced before. It still remains one of my most memorable dining experiences. It was incredible. The whole experience was beautiful and 4hrs later, after much laughter, many stories,

and a full stomach we were done! It was hard to go back to
fast food after that, I just wanted to save up and do it all over
again as quickly as possible!

You see, like my incredible dining experience, when you have
experienced a different level of the fullness of God, you want
to push into it for more and not less, because God has always
something new to say, he has always more insight, more revelation and his presence is so tangible that everything we ever
thought love looked like is realized in him. Love is a person,
it is Jesus himself.

There is an intimacy that God calls us to, a nakedness, a deep
place that requires incredible vulnerability, courage and sur-
render. It is a place where trust is cultivated and an excite-
ment at what will happen. How will we encounter Him tonight? How will he speak? What will be the song that will be
expressed and birthed tonight?

I was always surprised. Never did God not show up. Never
did we run out of songs. There was always fresh manna – I
mean new songs every week, different themes, different emphasis and different people bringing it.. You see, the thing I
have learned is, you must give space for God to move, you
must be intentional, hungry, being willing to wait, not in a
rush for anything – it's like waiting on the yeast to work into
the bread, it needs time to prove, to rise, then you can put it
into the oven – but you cannot rush the process, to do so will
result in a flatter bread, and you lose out on the end result of
goodness. In these times of worship, we waited, we listened,

tuned into where God was going because we wanted to follow where he was going.

It was from this place that not only a prophetic ministry grew, prophetic schools grew, but more importantly came a prophetic culture. A Culture which cultivated an environment of hope, encouragement and strength because it was undergirded with the knowledge of the goodness of God. My prayer as you read this book, is that you understand that all of us can hear the voice of God, and have a deeper friendship with him. Our journey in learning to hear God's voice and growing in our friendship with Him is one of no limitations, except those that we decide to put on ourselves. Pursue Him with all that you have, He does not disappoint, but will meet you in the middle of your search and your hungry heart.

DEVELOPING A PROPHETIC CULTURE

For as he thinks in his heart, so is he.

—PROVERBS 23:7 NKJV

If you've ever seen a skyscraper being built, you'll notice that the foundations have to go really deep. How high you can build depends on your foundation. It's the same with building a prophetic culture.

This goal of this book is to help lay a good foundation on which to build a prophetic culture—both as individuals and corporately as a Church.

WHO YOU ARE AND WHAT YOU THINK MATTERS

As Christians, our goal is to be bigger on the inside than we are on the outside. We want to be able to carry everything God has given us to carry. What I mean by that is, what are our core beliefs both about God and our own identity? I ask this, and see it as vitally important, because our thoughts shape everything. They shape how we respond to the world around us and the interactions we face every day.

And whenever God increases favor, authority and influence in our lives, we want a strong foundation to carry all those things, therefore, we increase our beliefs and values so they're healthy. We can build strong buildings on that foundation.

WHAT YOU BELIEVE ABOUT GOD MATTERS

What you think about God is the most important thought you're going to have. We come from so many backgrounds and so many different models of what we believe a father to be. If we have a model of a distant, cruel, angry father, we can project that model onto God and say, "Well, that's what God's like because that was my experience of a father." Your belief about God and your value for Him form the foundation you'll build on. Those beliefs and values will determine how you prophesy. Whatever is inside, will manifest outwardly, even those beliefs lodged in our sub-conscious that we are not aware of, but they affect how we live, interact and minister to others.

What is God like to you? Is He good? Is He angry? Is He distant?

Jesus came to put a face on God. And we're called to put a face on Jesus. In fact, the disciples were called "little Christs." We are called to model who we believe the Father is - and what we believe about Him will affect everything we do and say.

WHAT IS CULTURE?

Everyone is raised in a culture. A culture is simply a system of shared beliefs and values. Some of these beliefs and values are deeply held; some are never questioned or even spoken of. Even within your own family structure, you have a culture. In some families the unspoken culture is that everybody needs to know how to make Mommy happy. Everybody knows you don't speak about *that*. Our families create a certain culture because of what we believe and what we value. Everything will be affected, and the messages you receive will come through that culture. Think about a young couple getting married, they believe they are on the same page about everything until they start living together and until conflict comes. There are assumptions made by both parties, that because they are so in love and because they believe that God has brought this person into their lives it will be so easy! It can often be a shock to each person when they realize they don't share the same culture or values as they first thought, and then the real work of becoming one begins.

You have to work hard to build a strong prophetic culture. It requires working hard to grow, develop, and protect the prophetic culture you're building because it's such an important foundation. As a result, when you come into an environment or meet someone who has this in operation in their life, you *will* experience God's presence, His love and encouragement, and His hope.

When you enter an environment that carries a strong healthy prophetic culture, you will leave much more hopeful, more encouraged, because that is the very nature of God. He is a loving Father who wants to communicate to his children. You will believe that anything is possible.

As we change what we believe about God, we will see our lives changed.

WHAT ARE YOUR BIG ROCKS?

Stephen Covey wrote the book *The Seven Habits of Highly Effective People*. He uses a fantastic illustration he calls "big rocks." He fills a jar with sand, tiny pebbles, and water. When he tries to put in big rocks, he can't fit them in. When the jar is filled with the tiny things, there is no room for the big things. So Covey gets another jar and fills it first with big rocks—then with pebbles, then sand, then water. This way, everything fits.

The big rocks are your core beliefs and values—the way you see the world, the beliefs that determine how you act and live.

Here are some of my own personal big rocks:

1. **I believe that God is good:** He is a good Father, and He is good all the time. I remember growing up hearing that, "Yes, God is good, but sometimes, like a shepherd, He'll have to break your legs because He didn't want you to run away." I was always a bit confused by that! That didn't seem like a good shepherd to me. God is good, and He's good all the time.

2. **I have a high value for the Holy Spirit:** I will always make space in what I do for the Holy Spirit to move, whether ministering publicly or personally, building a friendship with Him. I love His presence, and I love when He honors us with His presence. Many churches take a position that if God moves sovereignly in our meeting, then all bets are off. Truthfully, I have not heard of any move of God that has not been preceded by people making room for God, giving time, making space and intentionally calling

on heaven. I really believe we need to be intentional in our pursuit of the Holy Spirit. What we honor will increase, and who we honor and value we make room for.

3. **I believe in a victorious eschatology:** What we believe about the end times will affect how we live. I believe that we are moving from glory to glory with increasing glory. Things are getting better and better, not worse and worse. You've heard that saying, "Things are going to hell in a hand basket." Well, the media would like you to believe that, and we are bombarded with messages telling us that every day. However, if you look at scientific research, you'll see that things are actually getting better. Things are better than they were a hundred years ago. As believers, we don't want to just hunker down until the end of the world and wait for Jesus to sweep us all away. We want to be in the world, bringing Jesus to people, and bringing hope where there is no hope. I honestly believe that the church does not understand the authority she walks in, and DOES NOT fully believe that God is really good. Instead of hiding and building bunkers, we need to understand Jesus has done everything and is waiting for us to do our part which is heal the sick, raise the dead and deliver people from their demons. All authority has been given to us, we do not have to wait on anything else happening!

4. **We are children of God:** You are not a worm. God didn't die for worms. He died for you because you are worth dying for. He loves you because you are worthy of His love. I think we have mixed up humility with low self-es-

teem. We are told to walk humbly, love God, thinking of yourself as nothing. However, denying the talent and good things God has gifted you with is NOT humility, it's low self-esteem, and at it's worst it is low lying self-hatred. When you walk in all that God has called you to, and in the joy of who you are, it brings Him glory, not us. "Shine your light before men, that they would see your good works and glorify your Father in heaven."Matt 5:16

5. **We are unoffendable:** We live judgment free. We don't make up stories about what people are going through, and we don't receive the stories people make up about us. We aim to be like Teflon pans, letting nothing stick— always walking in forgiveness. We don't do the accuser's job for him, but always believing the best about people and seeing them how the Father sees them. I think this is one of the biggest challenges for us to live without judging others harshly or even judging ourselves harshly. We live in a culture that rewards offence and cultivates it, but as lovers of God, it is so important that we move in love and not offence. It is a practice to stay unoffendable and an important area each of us to stay aware of.

6. **We create a culture of honor:** We embrace healthy relationships, and we are not afraid to navigate conflict. Honor is the ability to recognize someone, appreciate who they are, and not get focused on their flaws. I believe honor is crucial in our journey, not only in relationships, but in opening up more of the heavenly realm to us. If you can honor and value people, and what God has done in your life, you are opening the door to more. It keeps

your focus on what is happening and not on what isn't happening, and that will set you up for increase and acceleration,

7. **We live from Heaven to earth:** What would Jesus do in this circumstance? Finding the answer to that means going beyond how a circumstance looks to us and asking: How would Heaven see it? (Hint: Heaven is always filled with hope.)

8. **Living your identity as a Son or Daughter of God:** Jesus grew in favor with God and man. We must be teachable, adjustable, and correctable. I do believe this is connected with honor. Can you trust those in your life to adjust you? Can you receive feedback? Of course I am not talking about abusive leadership. Putting yourself under leadership who want to see you succeed. If you want to see the poverty Spirit broken off your life, and come into favor with God and man you will need to know what it looks like to be a son/daughter of God. If Jesus had to grow in these areas, then surely we have to as well.

WHAT YOU BELIEVE DETERMINES HOW YOU BEHAVE

Prophetic ministry will flow from a prophetic culture. Everything we minister will come out of the overflow of who we are. Out of the heart, the mouth speaks. Matt 24:12

We all carry a culture whether we are aware of it or not. What we carry, we will release—both good *and* bad. It's important that our inner world is focused on Heaven and the Father, the good and not the bad, on love peace and joy. All of us have experienced someone who was really angry and bitter because it overflowed in their conversation and their behavior. If you find yourself in the company of people who carry that culture like that, it will impact you, and not in a positive way either.

What about you? Is the culture you carry a good one? You will often find out in adversity. A while ago, the baby of a friend of ours died. Suddenly we were faced with the question: do we believe that God can raise the dead? Do we believe that God can heal? Yes and yes. As a result of that belief and value, we asked the parents if we could pray for their baby. We gathered and prayed. And though sadly we did not see the baby come back to life, that will not keep us from praying for resurrection. We don't always know why we didn't see it, but in the future because we believe that God still heals, and He has told us to raise the dead, I will continue to take those opportunities because Jesus through His death and resurrection, has given all of us the authority to do so.

That's the culture I carry. It's a culture of encouragement and strength. When you look at prophetic culture, it is one of *yes*. You get to add your amen to God's *yes*. You live under a green light, full of hope, expecting good things.

If that is not your culture, you can change it. It's not always easy, but with training, you can do it. And if you are reading this, it's a good indication that you are looking for growth and help to change.

In Proverbs 23:7 it says: "As man thinks, so he is." Take five minutes and think: what are your core beliefs about yourself? About God? Write them down. The results might surprise you.

THE LANGUAGE OF GOD

My sheep listen to my voice; I know them,
and they follow me.

—JOHN 10:27 NIV

This is one of my favorite topics because I love gathering testimonies of how God has spoken to people. I get excited and encouraged when I hear people's stories.

GOD WANTS US TO KNOW HIM
AND TO HEAR HIS VOICE

In John 10:14, Jesus says: "I am the good shepherd; I know my sheep and my sheep know me…." (NIV). Later in that same chapter, Jesus also says: "My sheep listen to my voice; I know them, and they follow me" (John 10:27 NIV). If we're following God's voice, we have to be able to hear His voice.

We all have the ability to hear the voice of God. God *wants* us to hear Him. He's not trying to trick us or hide from us. One of the stumbling blocks as we try to hear Him is the worry, "How do I know what I'm hearing is not just me? How do I know I'm not making this up?" That is one of the main questions I encounter, and we'll look at that a bit later.

As my husband, Ian, says: "We don't have a proximity problem. We have an awareness problem." It goes back to culture and beliefs—back to building an internal landscape for yourself. It's about changing your awareness to the truth that God is always with you.

OUR BIGGEST GOAL: FRIENDSHIP WITH HOLY SPIRIT

The Hebrew word for spirit is breath. God is as close as your breath. God is not way up there—He's right in *here*. In us.

Say you buy a car. You've never really noticed the make and model before, but since you just bought one, you now see that same car everywhere. It's a similar principle when you start to think from Heaven to earth. As you start to think that God *does* want a relationship with you and that He *is* as close as your breath—whether you feel Him or not—your awareness changes.

Our biggest goal in all of this is friendship with Holy Spirit. We want to know the character of God. If we can get over our own self-doubt, if we are childlike in believing God is who He says He is, we will see exponential growth.

A few years ago while we were going through a very difficult circumstance for a number of years, we had God continually speak to us about it, telling us through many trustworthy prophets and prophetic people that it will be fine. He told us that everything will be okay and that He was with us and to trust Him. For many years, our circumstances did not change, in-fact sometimes they even got worse, but we knew

God had spoken, we absolutely knew that God would bring us through.

When you have a word from God you can stand on it. When He has spoken, you have to believe it, test it, and let the word test you – but when it is from God there is a grace released with the word and it will sustain you. God is so good, and when we are in the middle of terrible battles, we get to see what we really believe about the goodness of God. We get to decide to stand on his words, and if we believe they are the truth or not. We always have a choice. I want to be immoveable when storms come, I don't want to have to decide what I believe about God in the middle of it. I want to be a friend of God, because sometimes the only thing that kept us going were His words to me and my family. They became an anchor that never moved and we fully believed and held onto. I can tell you having walked through this, it looks completely different. We watched our circumstances slowly shift, and today we are seeing those prophetic words unfolding in our lives and in the lives of our family. We carry a testimony to God's goodness and His faithfulness. If you find yourself in the middle of difficult circumstances, don't give up, because God wants you to know Him and His deep love for you in the middle of even the most painful of times.

As you begin to build a friendship and history with God, you learn to recognize Him. If a dear friend calls you on the phone, you don't need to ask, "Who is this?" It's the same with God. You build a friendship with Him, and everything will come from that friendship.

Sometimes we forget that it takes time to build a friendship and a history with God, it is something that cannot be imparted, but must be grown in us. It takes time, like any friendship. It is about pursuing God with ALL our hearts, going after everything he has for us. It's not about us waiting on something happening to us, it is about training our senses to recognize Him and to tune into how He speaks to YOU. If you think of all the friends you have, they are all different. I am sure they are all wired differently, they like different things, they have different taste in clothing, music, literature. It is the same with our friendship with God, we have access to this incredible person who loves us and wants us to know Him. We build a friendship with Him, that is so personal because He knows you better than anyone!! I believe this is the place we lose out or can become discouraged when we compare our journey and progress with others – that will always steal your joy. Comparison is the thief of joy. It is so important to enjoy our friendship with Him and let that grow over time.

This is all about being stronger and bigger on the inside than you are on the outside. When storms come, as they will, you will know that you know that you know God is always with you.

LEARN THE WAYS GOD COMMUNICATES WITH YOU

Long ago, I heard this phrase: "God's first language is not English." The mother tongue of Holy Spirit is encouragement. It's hope. It's love. It's faith. When we hear God's voice, it should always bring encouragement—even when He is adjusting or correcting us, His voice will always leave us encouraged.

Look at the disciples. They always felt better being around Jesus—even when He was adjusting them. The voice of Holy Spirit will always leave you feeling loved. In contrast to the voice of the accuser, which will always leave you feeling less. We have to remember that God is a good Father, and the devil is the accuser of the brethren. God never accuses, he does adjust us and corrects us, but not in a way that will destroy us, but will help us grow and have a better capacity for Him.

SOME WAYS GOD SPEAKS

God is so very big and there are so many ways He speaks. I'd like to share just a few ways that I and others I know have heard Him. There is so much more than this list, but this will get us started:

1. **Scripture:** Our plumb line is always Scripture. God will never speak outside of His own character. He will not speak contrary to who He is. You can be sure that God is not telling you to jump off a bridge—an extreme example, but you get my point. God will never speak to you in a way that diminishes you. He wants to increase you and see you grow. He wants to see you thrive and be abundant so that you can affect the people and world around you. For many people, Scripture is the main way they hear from God. Sometimes, people will hear God while reading Scripture—the written Word, the *logos*. Sometimes, people will hear the *rhema* word: the "now" word of God that jumps out at you as you read the page. I encourage you to know Scripture. When you know the Word of God, you understand the character of God. Scripture is alive, and anything that is alive is also interactive. The word of God strengthens us, it feeds us, and should always be our foundation of understanding who God is.

2. **Dreams:** This is one of the biggest ways I personally hear from God. I remember receiving dreams but having no one to talk to and not knowing what the dreams meant. I wasn't in an environment where the gifts of the Spirit were operating. Later, as I met other people and came into a better understanding of the gifts of the Spirit, I received more training, and through that I was able to understand that my many of my dreams were from God. We'll talk more about dreams later, but I'll share one here. I once dreamed that I was getting married to our worship pastor, and at the end of the dream, I awoke with a beautiful sense of God, there was a beautiful sense of love and presence of God, it was just an incredible feeling of joy . There was nothing weird about it, but at first I wondered what it could mean, because I was married and our worship pastor was a good friend, so it felt confusing at first so I asked the Father, "What did that dream mean?" I felt immediately he gave me the interpretation; the dream was about the marriage of worship and the prophetic. The marriage of those two produced a beautiful sweetness. I represented the prophetic and this friend was representing worship. The union of those two is part of my life message. It is truly the greatest area of joy and life for me. When those two pieces come together, it releases something very beautiful from Heaven, that is very powerful. So, don't write off your dreams. Pay attention to them. Write them down. Ask for interpretation. If you don't know the interpretation find people who can help you.

3. **Visions:** There are many kinds of visions. With external or open visions, you see something playing out in front

of you. You could be standing in the street, and it's like a movie is playing out. Then there are internal visions. These might look or feel like a ticker tape going across your mind, or you'll see something in your imagination. Scripture is full of visions. Sometimes they happen so quickly, we often dismiss them or think they are just from ourselves. As with all ways of hearing God, we need to pay attention. We can all hear Him, but we don't always attribute what we hear to Him. Remember that God is often more than not heard in the whisper – he doesn't shout that often, and we are so inclined to think, "Oh that was just me" and dismiss it, but increase your awareness, don't let it go, pay attention, because God is speaking more than we think or believe.

4. **Impressions**: When I'm driving, or just getting on with my normal day to day stuff, I often receive impressions. I'll think of a person and wonder how they are and think, "I should check in with them." Maybe you wake up in the morning and someone is on your mind or heart. That's the Father. He loves us so much, he will put people on our hearts and vice versa—usually to contact and encourage, or to pray for. A friend texted me the other day with a simple bit of gratitude, and it was so encouraging. Impressions can be simple but powerful. Pay attention to them. Sometimes I will think of someone and that day I will bump into them. God is often prompting us, and at times giving us insight to who is coming into our path on particular days.

5. **Trances**: Some of the revivalists used to go into trances. I personally have never experienced these. In Acts 10:10,

Peter fell into a trance. I wonder what that looked like! I don't know, but trances fascinate me. I know close friends who this has happened to and often it is an intimate time with God, where he speaks to them on something very specific. It really is incredible how God speaks to us and the different ways he chooses to do that, it's one of the reasons we should never limit our thinking around how He will choose to do it.

6. **Audible voice**: Moses heard it. Paul heard it. Jesus heard it at His baptism. I know people who have heard God's audible voice. A friend of mine went for a job interview. When he left and got into his car, God spoke to him and audibly said, "The job's yours." Back home, he received a phone call: he got the job.

7. **Hearing with the ears of your spirit**: One Sunday at church during worship, some of us heard another layer of sound. It was an angelic sound. We heard it not with our physical ears, but with the ears of our spirit. It was incredible, there were so many people who heard it, that we couldn't dismiss it as our imagination. Sometimes I have been sleeping and I have heard my name called as close as audible as it could be, but it wasn't audible, it was with my spirit, but it woke me out of my sleep. That has happened to me a number of times. Like Samuel, when God called him and it was so clear. Our Spirit has 5 senses, so we can hear, smell, touch, taste and see with our Spirit. We can train our senses.

8. **Angels**: Daniel, Mary, the shepherds, the disciples, Jesus—so many people in Scripture had angels minister to

them. I know people who've had visitations from angels. You might have heard stories of Muslims who've had angelic visitations and have come to Jesus—or have been visited by Jesus Himself, the Man in white. Sometimes you might have an angel come to you in a dream as a messenger, this is very normal, especially around important events that God wants to communicate to you about. We are surrounded by the Angelic, I believe it is a normal part of the Christian life, to expect encounters from these heavenly beings. Any encounter we have with the angelic, should always draw us closer to Jesus, because they love Him and adore Him so much, and carry the presence of Heaven with them.

9. **Creation**: Romans 1:20 tells us: "For since the creation of the world God's invisible qualities—his eternal power and divine nature—have been clearly seen, being understood from what has been made..." (NIV). I am deeply moved by beauty, especially creation and its majesty. We often take groups on retreat to Ireland with us, and without exception they are struck by the beauty of the land. When you walk in the mountains, it's impossible to not respond in worship to the Creator of creation. The land is alive with centuries of prayers, ancient prayers that linger still, hanging in the atmosphere, with their presence still felt if we have our senses trained to experience it.

10. **Prophetic words**: God speaks to us through his body. At times when we are in difficult circumstances, getting a prophetic word from a prophet or a prophetically gifted person can feel like a lifeline. Many times I have experi-

enced the encouragement and kindness of God through a prophetic word. Proverbs 25:11 "A word in the right season is like, Apples of gold, in settings of silver". A prophetic word, given at the right time and in the right season releases encouragement, comfort and strength to keep going and not give up. I have heard people say, "if God wants to tell me something, he will tell me himself" but really if we are the body of Christ, and we need each other, why would we not let God use others to speak to us. Throughout scripture, both in the Old and New Testament, it is a normal part of how God communicates his heart to us.

11. **Signs & Wonders & Miracles:** I've seen people healed right in front of me. I have watched as what can only be described as specs of glitter appeared many times on my husband as he spoke, they began to appear on his face, his shirt, his hands while he preached, and they had not been there before he got up to speak. One of the strangest signs I've ever seen was when a friend of mine received a gold tooth by going through a fire-tunnel. (This is really like a blessing tunnel, and as people go through it, those who form the tunnel ask for God to encounter those going through) The interesting thing was, she didn't even want it, she went through a fire-tunnel at church and when she came through it, her mouth felt like it was on fire, and when we looked, one of her teeth had become completely Gold. I have no explanation, I think it's a sign and a wonder, and as the Psalms says "God does as He pleases." I have seen people whose hands have been stiff with Arthritis and in pain, be completely healed. Terminally ill

people with Brain cancer, get healed. It is inspiring and such an encouragement for all of us to continue to pray for the sick and partner with God to see his Kingdom come. This is available for all of us.

12. **Normal, everyday things:** I love these. A lot of times, God will speak to me through street names. One time, Ian and I were driving to a conference. We got a bit lost. I looked up and saw a road sign for Pioneer Road. I told Ian, "I think this is prophetic." I don't think every street sign means something, but this one struck me. Over the next few years, we found ourselves pioneering something we had never expected to. Another time I was driving and I took a wrong turn. I saw a street sign which was my friend's name. It was a good friend from home in Northern Ireland, so I looked him up on Facebook and saw it was his birthday. This felt significant to me, so, I asked the Father if He had something for my friend, and He gave me a word of encouragement for him. I could have ignored the street sign, thinking it was a novelty, but because I paid attention and kept my awareness open, I followed it through and it really blessed my friend.

13. **Puns:** One other thing I have found is that God loves Puns! Who knew! He really is impossible to put in a box and assume he only moves in certain ways! We should never limit how we think about the ways God can speak to us. Be always looking, listening. The Father loves to play with us. If we are created to look and act like Him, and part of the fruit of the Spirit is joy, and He is a joyful God, you know He loves doing joyful things.

14. Friendship and the affections of God: Sometimes, interactions happen between God and I that no one else would understand, but I know He's speaking to me. God loves to interact with us personally throughout the day. This is a friendship. This is not about big God, little us. This is a big God who is amazing, who loves us, who wants to be known by us. This is God, who is as close as the air we breathe, as I said before, this is not a proximity problem, it's an awareness problem, and we need to train our senses to recognize and understand He is always with us and what that looks like.

It's fun to learn the languages of God. Most important is learning how God speaks to you, specifically. What patterns do you see again and again that you might have dismissed? God has been speaking to you for a long time. How God has wired you is how He will talk to you.

One of the biggest things that can trip us up is hearing stories of how others hear from God—different ways than we hear from Him. If we begin to compare, we can get discouraged. I have never heard the audible voice of God. I could let that discourage me, or I could remind myself that I've heard God speak to me in many other ways.

Stay encouraged, keep paying attention to how God *is* speaking to you, and remember that He is always speaking.

DREAMS

Indeed God speaks once,
Or twice, yet no one notices it.
In a dream, a vision of the night,
When sound sleep falls on men,
While they slumber in their beds,
Then He opens the ears of men,
And seals their instruction...

—JOB 33: 14-16 NASB

We've talked about the language of Heaven and how God speaks, and now we're going to talk about dreams. Certainly in my own life, dreams have been one of the strongest ways God has spoken to me. Maybe that's because I don't listen as well during the day, and He can more easily speak to me at night! But I find that time and time again, He speaks to me in dreams because He is a revelatory God. He speaks Spirit to spirit; Holy Spirit speaking to our spirit. And He drops things into our spirit at night that we're not always aware of. Remember our spirit does not sleep, so God can interact with us during our sleeping and we may or may not be aware of it.

We live in a logical world. A world where one plus one equals two. I don't think it works like that in the Kingdom. Sometimes with God, one plus one can equal ten. We have often used logic to remove the mystery of God. But God is mysterious; God speaks beyond our logic—He speaks in dreams, parables, metaphors, symbols. And He gives us the chance to work those things out—which can be quite fun.

As those verses in Job 33 remind us, God speaks to us in dreams. Job 33:15 "In a dream, a vision of the night. When sound sleeps falls on men while they slumber in their beds. Then He opens the ears of men and seals their instruction."

EXAMPLES OF DREAMS IN SCRIPTURE

All through Scripture, God speaks to people in dreams—even people who are not believers. The heart of God is that people would know Him and encounter Him.

In Daniel 2:1, we see God speaking to King Nebuchadnezzar in a dream. In Daniel 2:19, Daniel receives the interpretation of the dream. God then gives Nebuchadnezzar another dream—a warning dream—because the king had not been taking care of the poor or being merciful to them. Nebuchadnezzar did nothing about the dream, and, as God had spoken, he went insane for seven years.

Joseph was told by the Father in a dream that Mary was carrying the Messiah. Joseph had wanted to leave Mary; he was embarrassed that she wasn't married and now pregnant. Imagine that your fiancé comes to you and tells you she's pregnant with God's Son. You might need God to confirm that and he did that with Joseph in a dream.

In Matthew 1:20, Joseph had an encounter with an angel in his dream and was warned to return home by a different route.

In Matthew 2:12, the Wise Men were also told to travel a different route because Herod was going to kill all children under two years old.

In Matthew 27:19, Pilate's wife dreamed that she would suffer greatly if she messed with Jesus.

There are over 220 biblical references to dreams. God uses dreams for many different things. We could spend days on dreams; it's a deep topic. If you want to learn more, look into John Paul Jackson's Streams Ministry International.

We'll cover just a few elements of dreams in this book.

WAYS GOD USES DREAMS

God uses dreams for instruction, for warning, for salvation. As I mentioned, many Muslims have come to Jesus because He appeared to them in a dream. I personally know someone who dreamed that Jesus came in a dream, and this man gave his life to Him.

God can also give dreams of direction, to show you the next steps you need to take. There are dreams for strategy and solution.

At one point, my family and I were in a difficult spot. One morning, I had a short dream, a vignette on the brink of waking. Those happen often to me. I dreamed that my son and I were walking through the woods. He pointed out that in the woods, which was covered in snow, that a wolf was there and we to be careful. All of a sudden, a wolf emerged. He bared his teeth in a frightening way, but he didn't touch us.

Immediately, I woke up, and I knew the meaning of the dream. In the midst of all that we were going through as a family, the enemy was after us. He was trying to destroy us— that's his job: to kill, steal, and destroy. With the revelation of my dream, a righteous anger rose up in me. The enemy was not going to destroy my family. The Lord was showing me the bigger picture of what was happening. Seeing the enemy in my dream was a kind of strategy for me; I knew who was behind the difficulties, and that knowledge helped me fight. I went from being pretty discouraged, to being resolute that I would not be taken down by the enemy and that he would not have the last say!! It's amazing what can happen when God speaks, it changes everything.

Dreams are also another way for us to encounter the goodness of God. God brings encouragement through dreams. Sometimes this encouragement is for other people, and so you may have a dream for someone else.

Dreams can be about your calling. I mentioned the dream about marrying the worship pastor. It meant a marriage the prophetic to worship. I experience Holy Spirit the most in that place of the prophetic and worship, that calling dream marked me in a beautiful way.

Unfortunately, we can often dismiss dreams. You know how you awaken from a dream and it starts to dissipate? I try to write down the dream right when I wake from it. Even in the middle of the night, write it down so that you can re-member it. God is speaking; we don't want to miss it! There are times when I am in the middle of a dream and I realize it is a prophetic dream, and I don't write it down, because I am sure I will NOT forget it, but when I wake up, I have completely forgotten the details. So, I can't encourage you enough to write it down immediately.

There are different kinds of dreams:

1. **God dreams:** In these dreams, God brings you wisdom, a prophetic word for someone else, strategies, etc. These are dreams where the Father speaks to you in the night, and, like Job says, He seals His instruction.

2. **Soul dreams:** In these, our minds or souls are often processing events and trying to figure things out. These dreams can reveal underlying issues, especially conflict. A long time ago, a good friend and I had a disagreement, and we couldn't fix it. I didn't trust her, and she didn't trust me. We had been really good friends, but we just couldn't fix this. One night, I dreamed that I had twins, and she had one of my twins; she had the girl, and I had the boy, and she wouldn't give the girl back to me. That wasn't a God dream. That was me trying to resolve things. Emotional issues will show up in our dreams as our soul tries to work things out. They are still very helpful and can help us get resolution to issues we are not always aware of.

3. **Nightmare/crazy dreams:** The enemy can torment us in the night. To counter that, we need to grow in our authority as a Christian and understanding who we are. If you have a dream that you're being shot, and you're shooting back with just a water pistol, that could be about your authority needing to grow. When we wake from

these dreams, we often feel like we've been slimed. Don't be discouraged, but do press in and look for places you can grow in authority. It's also important to remember that we carry all the authority and the enemy only has any authority that we give to him. We give him authority when we believe lies about our identity, lies about God's goodness. When we hold unforgiveness and bitterness, we allow him access to torment us. Understanding the greatness of who is in us will change our lives.

4. **Encounter dreams:** These are similar to God dreams, but these involve visitations. Many friends and as well as myself, have had prophets show up in our dreams. When you wake from these you often wonder: did that really happen...or was it a dream? These are powerful and feel real—and good. One time, I had an angelic visitation in a dream. I was in the middle of the street, and I remember thinking: "This is an open vision!" Something was happening within my dream. I woke up feeling peaceful and surrounded by the presence of God. I really believe there are times we wake up from what we think is a dream and it has really been a heavenly encounter, but because we don't fully understand, or don't believe it, we just mark it as a nice dream.

DREAMS CAN OFTEN BE
ASSIGNMENTS OR ENCOUNTERS

Remember that your spirit doesn't sleep. Holy Spirit often interacts with us at night. Some people have even been taken to other countries while in their sleep, and have woken up thinking it was only a dream. I know people who have received emails from people in different countries, thanking them for coming to minister the previous night...while they were at home in bed asleep!

This of course has not been a dream but an assignment, and there are times we will be aware of the assignment and other times we will not, but we may find out at a later date from other people. There are times when you wake up feeling more exhausted than rested and that can be an indication you may have been on a night assignment.

I have had prophets show up in my dreams, but also, I have shown up and ministered to people in their dreams. I love that!

I have woken up some mornings from a dream, to realize it was most likely not even a dream, but a heavenly encounter. I remember one particular instance I woke up from what I thought was a dream, that was so vivid and beautiful, that when I woke I started to cry, I was so sad that it finished, because I had never experienced anything so beautiful before. All that day, when I thought about what I had seen I would feel God's presence and I found myself starting to weep, overwhelmed by the goodness of God.

These are mysteries I don't fully understand, but there is scriptural reference for them. I remind myself that God is not logical; He's mysterious. We don't have to understand everything, and we have to be willing to partner with God and not be afraid. If these things feel out of our experience, we can dismiss it, but the scriptures are full of strange things. The plumb-line for me is that when God speaks, when He interacts with you, when He gives you dreams or encounters, it should always increase your love for Him. It should bring you closer to Him or it should benefit others on their journey with Him. The experiences are not just for the sake of having amazing encounters, but they ultimately should lead us to know Him better.

GUARD YOUR HEART

I would suggest that as you start to pay attention to your dreams that you also guard your heart. Your heart is the well-spring of life. Be careful: if you need to put boundaries on movies you watch, what you look at, do so. There are some things I can't watch. I'm careful about that because I'm very sensitive to my environment. We have to pay attention to how we're wired, everyone is different and some people have wider parameters than others, we have to do what is best for us and not what others do.

WHY DOES GOD SPEAK IN RIDDLES?

Why doesn't He just make it plain and easy? I don't know, but I think it's because He will never remove our need for Him. I think God loves to keep the conversation going because He knows we'll enjoy it. He's given the gifts and ability to do so.

HEAVEN IS ATTRACTED BY HUNGER

Historically, every Jewish boy's dream was to be a rabbi. At the age of twelve, they would be selected to study with a rabbi not on the basis of their knowledge of the Torah but on the basis of what questions they asked—how well they could keep the conversation going. Remember when Jesus was in the Temple at age twelve? They marveled at his questions.

I think God loves our hunger. Hunger runs through all the prophetic—stay hungry. In 1 Cor 14:1 "Eagerly desire " that means to pursue with zeal, that is an active posture. Going after the Holy Spirit and what He wants to give us is really important.

If God spoon-fed us all the answers, we wouldn't stay hungry. Even the disciples asked, "Why do you speak to us in parables?" I think God wants to keep us hungry. And Heaven cannot resist a hungry heart.

So stay hungry and pay attention to your dreams.

DREAM INTERPRETATION 101

*It is the glory of God to conceal a matter;
to search out a matter is the glory of
kings.*

—PROVERBS 25: 2 NIV

This will be a basic overview, and if you're interested, you can do further study on your own.

About 80% of the time, your dreams are about you. They are largely symbolic; another person in your dream often represents a part of yourself. As I mentioned, God speaks to us in riddles because mystery sends us to Him to search out the meaning and keeps us hungry for pursuing Him. To solve the riddles, we will always need Him.

THERE IS NO FORMULA

This is not about dream analysis. This is not about A = B always equaling C. Because everything in your dream is in the context of *you*. So things will have different meaning for differing people. Take dogs. I love dogs, and I had a husky.

However, if you are terrified of dogs, and a dog shows up in your dream, the dog may represent something entirely different for you than it would for me. It's always about context, context, context. And it's always about going to Holy Spirit and asking: What is this dream about?

Dreams can be interpreted immediately—even as they unfold. Some dreams require more processing. If you write the dream down and look at all the parts, you might start to see what it means. God might hold the meaning from you—not necessarily forever but until the right time. There may be an unfolding in your own process.

You may dream a series of dreams about your calling, but God might not reveal the meaning to you until you mature into them. Hold onto those dreams. There is no formula for dreams. It's about being in a relationship with the One who brings revelation.

A dream's meaning might be literal. A long time ago, I went for a job interview and I dreamed that I got the job. A few days later, I received a phone call saying I had, indeed, got the job. That's a literal interpretation.

A dream might be symbolic or allegorical. When Joseph dreamt about the seven fat cows and the seven skinny cows, the dream wasn't about cows; the cows symbolized years of abundance and famine.

Some dreams might be obscure. God may hold the meaning of these for a while, and you may need to go searching or keep holding onto these dreams until He reveals their meaning to you.

John Paul Jackson said that dreams can be like editorial cartoons from Heaven. They say more than just the simple things we can see.

HELPFUL POINTERS FOR DREAM INTERPRETATION:

1. What is the dream about? Are you in the dream? What are you doing in the dream? Are you watching what's happening or participating in it? If you are participating in the dream, the dream is usually about you.

2. Reduce the dream to its simplest form. There are often many elements in dreams, but if you can simplify the dream and find a couple sub-focuses, you can more easily understand it.

3. Write down the main elements. Colors? Objects? People? Animals? Different animals can represent certain things—though, as I mentioned, those things will vary in personal meaning. Context is important.

4. What are your thoughts in the dream? Are you afraid? Peaceful? Excited? When you wake up, what do you feel about the dream?

5. Was the dream in color? Black and white?

6. Was it a prophetic dream?

7. Was it a soul dream? Were you trying to work out a current issue?

8. Was it just a crazy dream?

9. If it was a God dream, was it a calling dream? A dream of the future? A strategy dream?

10. What would you title your dream?

11. Always ask Holy Spirit to help—both to remember your dreams and to interpret them. You can ask Him for the gift of interpretation.

Sometimes we have the tendency to believe the gifts of the Spirits just happen to us. We might believe we either have them or we don't, but that is not the case, we need to grow in everything God has given us. We want to be able to hear God and interpret what He is saying. With training, experience, and Holy Spirit, you'll be build up the ability to interpret dreams. It's like building a muscle. I have found it to be a lot of fun learning in this whole arena, there are many different resources for you if you want to learn more.

You can also ask people with more experience. I have a good friend who has interpreted thousands of dreams, and she understands dream language. If I get stuck, she'll help me with an interpretation. That's why we're in a Church Body; we can help each other.

Here's an example of a dream. A woman dreamt that a lady named Ann came to her door with a bouquet of flowers. The woman who answered the door leaned over to smell the beautiful fragrance of the flowers. But when she went to thank Ann, Ann was gone. When this woman awoke, she looked up the name "Ann." The name means the grace of God. At the time, this woman was going through a hard time. The dream was a representation of God's grace. God was telling her: I'm with you and my grace is with you.

God likes to use wordplay in dreams, too. A friend of mine dreamed that she was riding on a train and instructing someone. We took the different pieces of the dream and broke them down, looking for what God was saying. We realized that she was called to train others—and in the dream she was on a train. God used a play on words, a pun, as part of a dream of calling. He has a wonderful sense of humor.

COMMON DREAM ELEMENTS AND THEIR COMMON INTERPRETATION

In dreams, some elements can often represent the same thing—though again, I want to caution you that there are no hard and fast rules. Water doesn't always represent Holy Spirit. But it can.

There are many common dreams. If you've dreamed you were flying, those are often fun. Those dreams can mean you are moving with or going higher with Holy Spirit. Dreams of breathing underwater can also be connected with Holy Spirit.

Back to dogs. In the Bible, dogs aren't always spoken of in a great way. But in our culture, dogs are often a man's best friend. And if you like dogs as I do, a dog could be a good thing in a dream. It's always about what's going on with the dreamer.

People often dream of houses, which can represent your life. If you dream about the attic, that can represent your past memories. If you dream about a basement, it could be that there is something in your foundations you need to look at. If you're on the front porch, it could mean you are looking to the future. If you're on the back porch, it might refer to your past.

Numbers and colors might recur in your dream, for example if you see a house and the number 444 and you have other dreams, where the same number appears it could be significant. It might be a scripture verse, or reference something else that means something to you personally. If you're on a bike or in a car—or in some mode of transport—that can often refer to your ministry. Is the car stopped? Is it moving? Are you driving? Are you a passenger watching someone else drive?

It's fascinating. Practice interpreting your dreams. . I highly recommend that if you can, bring your dreams with a group of people you trust, friends who may have some experience in interpretation, or who love the prophetic, and discuss your dreams and see if they can help you interpret them, I think in community is a great way to bring a perspective that you might not have or see yourself.

Write down your dreams, break them down into their simplest forms, and ask, "What do you think God was saying at the time?" People will see things we don't see in our own dreams.

Practice. And pay attention to the details.

Before I end this section, I'd like to pray an impartation that God would give you dreams and visions and encounters in the night.

Father, I thank you for the hunger in this reader's heart. I thank you that they are building in the spirit.

Right now, I ask Father that you would release an impartation of dreams and visions and encounters in the night with you. Release dreams that would bring revelation to their calling, to their future, that would bring strategies.

I believe that God will release strategies to you in your dreams, that He will give you blueprints for what you are going to build, and that will be part of your calling. I pray increase upon increasing in dreams and visions and encounters. In Jesus' name, Amen.

GIFTS OF THE SPIRIT

*No longer do I call you slaves...but I have
called you friends....*

—JOHN 15:15 NASB

In the New Testament, we find different lists of the gifts. Romans 12 lists a whole ream of gifts of the Spirit, and those are often called the gifts of the Father or motivational gifts.

Ephesians 4 lists the gifts of the five-fold: the gifts of Jesus to the Church for the equipping, and maturing, and building up of the saints: the apostle, prophet, evangelist, pastor, teacher.

I Corinthians 12 lists the gifts of Holy Spirit. Those are the gifts we are going to focus on here, especially the gift of prophecy. But before that list, Paul writes this: "Now concerning spiritual gifts, brethren, I do not want you to be unaware" (I Corinthians 12:1 NASB).

This is an important piece for Christians. We need to understand these gifts. Verse 4 clarifies: "Now there are varieties of gifts, but the same Spirit." The word translated as "gift" here is the Greek word, *charisma*, which means "empowerment." God wants to empower us.

I've heard people say, "I want the Giver, not the gifts." I understand that, but it's a bit of false humility and it really doesn't make sense. If you want the Giver, then you also the things He wants to give you. I've also heard people say that they want the fruit of the Spirit, but they don't want to be greedy. God says He doesn't want us to be ignorant. Remember: when we are pursuing the gifts, they are not for us. Sure, we get to enjoy them, but it's not about us; the gifts are for building up the Church. Why would you not want to do that?

Let's skip the false humility. It's good to want both the fruit of the Spirit and the gifts of the Spirit—the whole shebang! You're not being greedy; you're being obedient. I encourage you to pursue Holy Spirit and His gifts with enthusiasm.

If, as a Mom, I give my children gifts and they refuse them saying, "No, I just want you," I would be devastated. I want to give them something that will help them and be good for them and I know they will love.

God wants to empower us, and He gives all gifts freely. Romans tells us that the gifts are given without repentance. As we move in the gifts of the Spirit, we might assume that we have amazing character because God has given us these gifts, but these gifts are not rewards for being good boys and girls. God has given these gifts freely to the Church for the benefit of the Church.

In I Corinthians 12: 7-12, Paul talks about the revelatory gifts of wisdom, words of knowledge, faith, and healing, miracles, discernment, tongues, and interpretation of tongues. Everyone has different gifts, but each gift is part of one Spirit, one Church Body and they are for that Body. Holy Spirit gives these gifts as He wills, and each gift is given according to the measure of one's faith.

Sandwiched between these gifts and the gifts of I Corinthians 14—which talks about prophecy—is love. Paul says love is the better way. Love has to be the foundation of everything we do, otherwise we're just clanging symbols making a lot of noise but not producing anything substantial.

Love is our foundation.

WHAT IS PROPHECY?

I think of the prophetic like an umbrella, and all the gifts are under that. Words of knowledge, words of wisdom, words of revelation, discernment, prophecy—prophetic words can have all of those components in them.

In I Corinthians 14:1, Paul talks about the importance of pursuing the gift of prophecy. What is prophecy? At its very core, it is hearing and communicating the heart and mind of Jesus. It's not complicated.

If I am the ambassador of a country, I need to represent that country well. If I am traveling to other countries, I need to know the heart of my home country. We are representing the Father, and we need to represent Him well. When we are prophesy over people, they are vulnerable; they are putting their hearts in front of us, and we must be gentle with those hearts—just like the Father would.

BECOME A FRIEND OF GOD

To hear God, we must be a friend of God. As John 15:15 says, we are no longer slaves; we are friends. That's the key; God is looking for friends—people He can trust who know Him and are known by Him. This is the heart of prophetic ministry.

Jesus modeled a friendship with God we can have. When you think of the language of Heaven, God wants to burst into our time and space to talk with us. Jesus called Himself the Word because He's always talking. The difficulty is that we are not always listening. We must increase our awareness of what God is saying and what is on the Father's heart that we can communicate well.

Think of long-term relationships in your life—friends or spouses you've known for years. When you hear their voice on the phone, you know who they are. They don't have to say their name. You recognize their voice, and you know them because you have built a relationship with them, you have built a history with them. In fact, you've probably spent so much time with them, you can finish their sentences.

Becoming a friend of God is as simple as that: spending time with Him to be able to hear Him and communicate His heart. When we move in the gifts of the Spirit, it's always for others. The only gift God gives us to build ourselves up is the gift of tongues; that's our own prayer language. Although, God can also give us a tongue (spiritual language) for corporate gatherings, and in my experience, He will give someone an interpretation for that. All the other gifts are for the common good—to build up the Body.

Our job is to make Jesus famous and to represent Him really well. His gifts are for the taking, and we can ask God for as many gifts as we want. When we pursue these things, it's to see people delivered, healed, and raised from the dead—and to see Jesus get what He paid for.

If you pursue all the gifts, it is likely that one will arise most strongly in you. For me it was the gift of prophecy. I love praying for healing, evangelizing, going after words of knowledge, etc. But I've really had a passion for the gift of prophecy; it's the gift I'm most hungry for. So I've trained in it and studied everything I could about it. I have read so many books, attended many schools, gone after impartations, and gathered people who are just as hungry for the prophetic, in-order that I could grow in this gift.

I encourage you to try all the gifts. Ask God: Can I have these? See what stirs your hunger. We don't know how far we can go. There's no limit. How hungry are you?

In our relationship with God, there never comes a time when we say, "That's it. I'm all good. I don't need any more of You." There are always layers to our friendship with Him, and it's the same with the gifts of the Spirit. The minute we think we have a handle on a gift, we'll discover other facets of it.

If Holy Spirit gives according to the measure of our faith, what if we keep increasing our faith? I Corinthians 14:1 tells us to pursue the gifts. That word "pursue" means to pursue with great zeal—to burn with zeal. Desire this thing so much that you will chase it down. There is nothing passive about the process. This is active pursuit of the things God has for you.

In our lives if we want to gain something we will invest in it in every way. It's the reason many people have a lot of student debts. They made a choice to grow in the area they wanted to pursue, and so they had to go to College. That's normal, it's assumed if you want something, you have to pursue it. It really is no different with your spiritual life. It is a pursuit of

God, you may need to invest in what God has called you to. It will cost you in time, money and energy, but with God there are no limits on what it will look like, because our pursuit of HIM will pay incredible dividends. Everything we walk in, comes from our relationship with HIM. The secret to any success is cultivating a friendship with God. I don't know of any other way. As I read about and look at people I love and respect, those who are further down the road than I am, I see, always at the core of their life is the pursuit of a friendship with God. They have usually paid a high cost to be where they are with God.

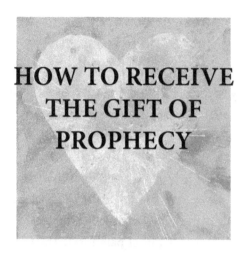

HOW TO RECEIVE THE GIFT OF PROPHECY

For I long to see you so that I may impart some spiritual gift to you, that you may be established....

—ROMANS 1:11 NASB

And when Paul had laid his hands upon them, the Holy Spirit came on them, and they began speaking with tongues and prophesying.

—ACTS 19:6 NASB

Do not neglect the spiritual gift within you, which was bestowed on you through prophetic utterance with the laying on of hands....

—I TIMOTHY 4:14

ARE THE GIFTS FOR ME? IF SO, HOW DO I RECEIVE THEM?

The gifts of the Spirit are free, not rewards. The most common way to receive a gift of the Sprit is by impartation from someone already moving in that gift. They come by the laying on of hands as we see in Scripture.

You can also ask God for the gifts. As I mentioned, I Corinthians 14:1 tells us to pursue the spiritual. Part of our job as people of the Spirit is to pursue the spiritual realm—to pursue the spiritual realities, especially prophecy.

The Kingdom is full of paradoxes. The first will be last. When you're strong, you're weak. The more you eat, the hungrier you get. We get to choose how hungry we want to be—knowing that the more we eat, the hungrier we'll get. This is an upside-down Kingdom, and I love that. It's mysterious. It's Heaven to earth.

HOW DOES THE GIFT OF PROPHECY GROW?

Say you've had someone lay hands on you to receive the prophetic gift. In most cases, God gives you a seed—your gift. As you nurture that seed and grow your experience, God will bring the increase.

God marks some people from a very young age, and they have a different kind of walk with Him. I've met people who have had experiences with Holy Spirit at six months old, and they remember it. That's more the exception. Most of us need training. In fact, even those who've had unusual experiences as young children still need training. We all need to develop our character—our inner landscape—so that we are strong enough to carry the calling on our lives.

If someone gave you a rifle and you didn't know how to use it, you'd be dangerous with it. However, if you were trained in how to use it, you could become a marksman, skilled in your craft. It's similar with the prophetic; If you don't learn how to use your gift well, you could hurt people, and many of us have had varying degrees of experiencing harsh prophetic words, or insensitive prophetic words. We want to build people up, not tear them down.

Your spirit has all the senses that your physical body has. Your spirit can touch, hear, smell, etc. Your responsibility is to train those senses. How do you train your spirit to hear God and be aware of His presence?

Scripture tells us that we need train our senses: "But solid food is for the mature, who because of practice have their senses trained to discern good and evil" (Hebrews 5:14 NASB).

Scripture also tells us the importance of discipline:

"All discipline for the moment seems not to be joyful, but sorrowful; yet to those who have been trained by it, afterwards it yields the peaceful fruit of righteousness" (Hebrews 12:11 NASB).

"Discipline yourself for the purpose of godliness" (1 Timothy 4:7b NASB).

The words for discipline in those Scriptures is *gymnazo*. It means to train vigorously. This is not a passive activity. We are responsible to train ourselves, to be educated in the school of the Spirit, and to be able to discern good from evil.

Essentially, we take our gifts to the gym. I used to do CrossFit. When I began, I could maybe lift 40 pounds. As I continued to train, I could lift 60 pounds. Then I deadlifted 100 pounds. Eventually, I could lift 180 pounds. I could not lift 180 pounds the first day I walked into that gym. I trained into that strength. It's similar with the gifts of the Spirit. We practice, practice, practice. We grow our gifts and our faith.

With practice, each time you can do something you haven't done before, you'll get more and more encouraged to keep practicing, to keep stepping out. The currency of the Kingdom is faith. You don't know how far you can go. You just keep building your reps. There is no limit. This is very exciting to know we are limitless in our walk with God. Imagine that depending on your hunger and desire, will depends on how deep you go with God. This is a partnership, as I said previously, this is not passive in any way, we have responsibility in this friendship to show up as best we can.

PRACTICAL DEVELOPMENT IN THE PROPHETIC

I Corinthians 14:3: "But the one who prophesies speaks to people for their strengthening, encouraging and comfort" (NIV). Every believer can prophesy, encourage, comfort and strengthen. Prophecy is for everyone because it builds the body up. On that level, prophecy is more about encouragement; it's not directional or correctional.

I think of the next stage as prophetic gifting—those are just words I've put to it to help clarify. When you begin to move in and practice the gift of prophecy, the prophetic gifting will start to emerge in your life. You'll start to have dreams and impressions on a more regular basis. As you grow in your gift, keep trying everything: pray for healing, pray for miracles. As I pursued the prophetic, I began to move in the gift of prophecy. As I grew in my gift, I received interpretation of dreams and words for people on a regular basis. And I stayed hungry.

If you keep moving forward, you'll see progression— though the prophetic is not about reaching one stage before moving on to the next. It's more an art than a science. Lines of progress are blurry, and it is not always a linear process.

Many people who move in the gift of prophecy equip others, though they may not be prophets. For me, people began to recognize things in my life before I had even had language for any of it. My passion was to equip people and raise them up to hear the Father's voice. That's what the prophet does: equip and mature the Church, bringing alignment, and unity.

A word of caution: When you're moving in revelatory gifts, people will begin to want you for your gift. And if you can't minister in that gift, you might feel like something's wrong. Remember that you are not the gift; the gift is something God has given us, but it is not our identity. Our identity is being a son or daughter of God.

There is a difference between being a prophet and being someone who moves in a prophetic gift. And this is all about serving others and calling them into their true identity as sons and daughters of God.

If you are in a church where the gifts are acknowledged, wonderful. If you're not, it can be difficult and harder to grow. We need to grow our gifts in a safe place—a kind of greenhouse. As we practice, we'll fail miserably, and we need to be able to be adjusted and trained in a safe place. As you move forward on this continuum, you might discover that you are a prophet. That's a whole different call. The prophet is the gift, and their life is the message. Often, this role is called out and acknowledged by others. It is always acknowledged by Jesus, the one who confirms all of the gifts. You can't decide to be a Prophet, and it's not a progression of doing all your training and then your final destination is to be a prophet. That is a different call and carries a different emphasis and responsibility to the Body of Christ.

As you begin in the prophetic, you can easily merge your own words with God's words. When you start to give prophetic words, it might be 10% God's words and 90% your words. We want to shift that percentage. Scriptures tells us to test all things and hold fast to what is good. So don't be afraid to make mistakes.

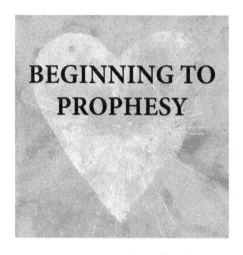

BEGINNING TO PROPHESY

For you can all prophesy in turn so that everyone may be instructed and encouraged.

—I CORINTHIANS 14:31

I come from Ireland. When you learn to drive there, you learn on a stick shift. When I started, I thought I would never remember everything… mirror, signal, maneuver, gears; who's in front of you, behind you, beside you; what's your speed? It's overwhelming when you are first learning. But as you keep practicing, it becomes second nature. You become familiar with what was once unfamiliar. Things become automatic.

When you first begin to move in the gift of prophecy, it can feel similar: There is so much to remember, and you're so conscious of yourself and others around you, and what if you make a mistake…?

I'd like to encourage you. (Remember: prophecy is for encouragement!) And as you practice and gain experience, the prophetic will become second nature.

When you begin to prophesy, you're sensitizing your spirit to Holy Spirit. Don't be afraid to ask Him: "Holy Spirit, make me sensitive to You." I try to pray that on a daily basis.

THREE COMPONENTS TO A PROPHETIC WORD

1. **Revelation:** You stand in front of someone and ask the Father: what do You see? He might give you an impression, an image, a thought, a Scripture. Use that as a springboard. That's the revelatory part.

2. **Interpretation:** This is about understanding what the revelation means. Say you see someone, and, in your mind's eye, God gives you a picture of a crossroads. You would tell that person, "I feel like you're standing at a crossroads." Then you might see them taking one of the roads. Your interpretation is what you think that picture is saying.

3. **Application:** What do you do with the information you've just been given? If the interpretation isn't right, the application won't be right. Sometimes you might know what the revelation means, other times you might not. And if you don't know what it means, don't feel under pressure to interpret. But if God gives you the meaning, you can proceed with the application.

These three components often happen almost simultaneously with a prophetic word. As I mentioned earlier, the prophetic is like an umbrella, and it can include words of wisdom and other elements as you prophesy and release revelation from the Father. Like dream interpretation, prophetic ministry is not a science. It's not a linear set of steps.

The prophetic gives you insight into a person's true identity. The Father will show you how He sees people. That's our goal: to see what the Father sees in someone and to encourage that identity and destiny. Ask yourself: how can I encourage this person? What is the Father saying about them? We want to communicate what He is saying—not our opinion.

I like to think of it like this. Say you're a mailman/woman. You have access to the post office and to the people's mailbox but you have nothing to do with what is in the letters; you cannot take credit for it, but you have access to them. Your job is to pick up the post and bring it to the people's door. Your job is to be a servant, serving the people, passing on what has been sent to them. When people receive an incredible letter, or a huge check in the mail, you have had nothing to do with it, only the delivery. Our job is very similar, we get to bring what God is saying to strengthen others. We want to represent Him well.

The worst thing you can do is "read" people. That's not prophetic. The prophetic is hearing what *Heaven* is saying about a person—not what we think about them. When Samuel went to Jesse's sons anoint a king, he went through all the handsome, tall brothers. But God kept saying, "No, no, no." Samuel asked if Jesse had any more sons; Jesse had disregarded the son God had chosen. Heaven sees people differently than we do. 2 Cor 5:16 (nasb)"Therefore from now on we recognize no one according to the flesh; even though we have known Christ according to the flesh, yet now we know Him in this way no longer. Therefore if anyone is in Christ, he is a new creature; the old things passed away; new things have come."

We are given strict instructions that we are to no longer see people as they are, but how the Father sees them.

Prophecy releases Kingdom identity. God sees who we truly are—and we want to communicate that truth.

It's also important how we prophesy, not just what we prophesy. People are often vulnerable when they allow you to see their heart and prophesy over them. We must be gentle and kind. If God can trust you with His children, He will give you more.

It's such a privilege to prophesy God's heart. We want to do so with honor.

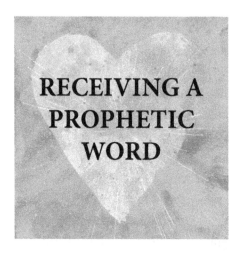

RECEIVING A PROPHETIC WORD

And we also thank God continually
because, when you received the word
of God, which you heard from us, you
accepted it not as a human word, but as
it actually is, the word of God, which is
indeed at work in you who believe.

—I THESSALONIANS 2:13 NIV

When someone gives you a prophetic word, it's important
how your receive that word. Prophetic words are conditional, they require your participation, and you aligning yourself
with the word, they are not absolute. There is only one absolute prophetic word given in the Old Testament and that
was about God bringing a Messiah, Jesus coming as Saviour.
But, in general, prophecies are conditional and they speak to
potential.

WHY DID THE OPPOSITE THING HAPPEN?

Sometimes when a prophetic word is released, the opposite happens. I've experienced this; I've received a future prophetic word I thought was amazing, and I anticipated it—but then the opposite started to happen. Once, we received a prophetic word about finances, and then all of our appliances started to break down. Every single month something broke down: the washing machine, the cooker, the fridge. And we had no money to replace them. It was crazy. Here, God had promised us one thing but the opposite seemed to be happening. We couldn't figure it out. That wasn't necessarily the devil.

It's important to realize that when prophetic words are released, it is so encouraging, it is positive but, after the word is released, things can start to go in the opposite direction, and it is in that place it is important what you do with the prophetic word. The word needs to be tested and built on the inside of us—especially when it's a word about our destiny or calling. We can mistake this strengthening process for the devil. It could be—but it could also be part of the process that gets you ready to lift bigger. Many times we have to contend for our word for the outcome to be positive and come to pass, So an important thing to remember that this is not unusual if it this happens – Positive, negative, positive seeing the word fulfilled.

Look at Joseph. He dreamed that the moon and stars and his family would bow down to him…. And then he was thrown in a pit and later into prison. Not exactly what he was expecting! Similarly, God called Moses to release the children of Israel into freedom, and then they all ended up in the desert for forty years. David was anointed king, but the throne wasn't his for twenty years.

How do we respond to the process of the word being built in us? Do we say, "Oh, that wasn't God," or "I'm going to pray into and prove this word."

Don't be discouraged if a prophetic word's trajectory goes from positive to negative to positive.

Say God has promised that you will help finance the Kingdom, but the week after you receive that word, you go broke. What are you going to do? Will you choose to believe this is a word from God? Will you choose to stand in faith and built your faith?

It's all a process of God building us up.

PLACING VALUE ON A PROPHETIC WORD WILL GIVE IT MORE POWER

The value you place on a prophetic word will determine the power you receive from it. If you dismiss it and don't invest in the word, it probably won't happen—the prophetic word is conditional. Some people take the attitude that it will magically happen, but I have not found that to be the case. We cannot be passive with our prophetic words, especially if there is a part that requires us to act on it.

Record everything. If someone prays or prophesies over you, record it. Get your smart phone and turn on the microphone. I normally won't prophesy over anyone unless they are recording it because I don't want to waste my words, and I want people to remember what God has for them. I also want to be accountable when I give a word. If a thing doesn't happen, I want to know so that I can make adjustments.

Record words *and* write them out—especially from seasoned prophets. Start declaring those words over your life.

Start investing in the words. I keep a folder of words I've received, and on winter Wednesdays, I'll open my folder and remind myself of my prophetic words. It's so encouraging.

Also: pay attention to elements of the word. Are you being called to action? Is there something you need to do? Is there something about your identity or calling? Say someone prophesies that you will be raised up as a worship leader who will sing songs that go to the nations. Well, what are you doing with that word? I hope you're singing. I hope you're writing songs. If you don't know how, are you going to take singing lessons? Taking a writing class? Connecting with a worship community? It's so important that we get prepared for when the opportunity comes, and if we are not, how can we step into it? God needs us to partner with Him. We all know the exceptions, the people who God gave an ability to speak a new language in a moment, or someone getting prayer and suddenly they can play the piano, but truthfully that is the exception rather than the rule.

We can often remain passive and think: "Well, if God said it, it will just happen." That's not how it works. Prophecy is potential; it won't necessarily happen. If you don't invest and follow through, then God will not be able to follow through with the prophetic word. We have a responsibility to what God has called us to.

Of course, there are things we have no control over. If you receive a prophetic word that God is going to put you before kings, you can still prepare. In our classes, we often ask, "What would you do if Oprah came in the room? What might the Father say to her?" You can practice that. You can ask God for words on a regular basis, so that when you do meet someone in a position of royalty or power, you will be able to release a word to them.

Take responsibility for your gift and be active in pursuing it with zeal.

Comedian Jerry Seinfeld worked for years and years in dingy comedy clubs with audiences of 15 and 20. He worked and worked until he reached a level of mastery. Mastery doesn't come overnight.

We are responsible to hone our craft, to stay hungry, to build up on the inside. Imagine what might your gift might look like after twenty years of practice?

PROTOCOLS & PITFALLS

Get wisdom, get understanding;
do not forget my words or turn away
from them.

—PROVERBS 4:5

Our goal is to learn to hear God as clearly as possible.

We need to receive feedback as we're learning. We need to be adjustable—and to have people in our lives who can adjust us. That's a large component of being a son or a daughter of God, which requires us like Jesus to grow in favor with both God and man. If we're not adjustable, we're scary. As Danny Silk would say, "Don't be scary."

HOW YOU RESPOND TO FAILURE IS IMPORTANT

If someone refuses to be adjusted, they can't be trusted to minister. As a leader, I would not have anyone on my team who refuses correction.

Mistakes will happen, but it's important how we respond to mistakes. If you have perfectionist tendencies, don't beat yourself up. Keep trying.

We don't have to be super talented, we just have to keep going—to not give up. God doesn't expect us to be perfect, but He does expect us to persevere.

I remember when my husband, Ian, was driving once, and he kept hitting red lights. He told God, "I'm hitting every red light!" God answered, "Yes, but you're going to get there anyway. You might get there a little later, but you'll still get there."

Just keep going. And when you do make a mistake, be willing to clean up your mess. Admit to your part and be accountable.

COMPARISON IS THE THIEF OF JOY

Don't compare yourself. As Theodore Roosevelt said: comparison is the thief of joy. It's like comparing a water bottle to a chair; those are two different things with two, different functions. God has wired us all uniquely, and we all have different levels of faith: "We have different gifts, according to the grace given to each of us. If your gift is prophesying, then prophesy in accordance with your faith..." (Romans 12:6 NIV).

When you hear Shawn Bolz, or Cindy Jacobs, or Kris Vallotton who are seasoned prophets, it can be easy to compare yourself to them. But we're all at different places with different gifts. We start where we are and build with what we have. If you can honor, and value what God has given you, be thankful for the small pieces you are aware of, then you will grow. It is so important where you focus, because whatever you direct your intention to and your focus on will become dominant in your life and that is positive or negative, but we get to choose. Also, many of the people we see in public and who have a large platform have spent years and years working and building, when no-one has seen it, but they have been faithful with what God has given them. We just see the highlights with no idea of what the cost, the time and sacrifice it has been to them and also to their family. Most of the people we admire, have paid a high price that we may never know anything about, and my guess is that their hunger has been to see the Kingdom of God advanced and not to be famous at all.

Just because someone is gifted doesn't mean God has endorsed their style. If you see someone moving in the prophetic in a certain style, you'll often see that the people they raise up will adopt the same style. Just remember everyone's style is different. Don't think you have to be a certain way to move in any of the gifts. You get to be you. Be yourself.

The gift is not the reward; it is a gift.

Stay focused on the Father. Don't strive to get a prophetic word. The more relaxed you are, the easier it is to hear God. When you're really stressed and under pressure, it can close you up. Personally, if there's a line of people in front of me, I feel pressured, sometimes you feel the responsibility is all yours and it's not, I have to remind myself to turn my focus back to the Father. Remember you are just the mail person who has access to the both people and also to the Post Office.

HOW DO YOU COMMUNICATE?

With love, love, love. Keep love as your foundation. When you prophesy, you rely on people's hunger. I was recently visiting a church with some of my team, and we could feel the hunger in the room. We could feel people pulling on our gifting. We want to go where the hunger is. People's hunger pulls on our gifting—it's fascinating.

INDIVIDUAL WORDS

If you feel that God has given you a prophetic word for an individual, it's a bit different. Make sure to record it. Don't do it in secret. You can even bring someone with you for your own accountability. By accountable, I mean they can listen and give you feedback later. Also, if you're a guy prophesying over a girl, having someone else present can be wise.

CORPORATE WORDS

If you feel that God has given you a prophetic word for a church, it's really important to always submit that word to the leadership. When you submit a word to leaders, you might expect them to release that word right away, but once you've submitted a word, your part is actually over. You've released the word. It's on the leader to release it or not. Even if they get it wrong, it doesn't matter; you've been obedient.

Different churches have different protocols for releasing prophetic words. In our church, Greater Chicago Church, when people have a prophetic word or song, they approach the leadership and share it, and the leadership will decide if and when to release it. You have to remember that the leaders are responsible for what is happening in the service, they more than likely have the big picture and if they don't let you share your word or song, then how we respond to "No" is just as important, actually if not more important.

DON'T PROPHESY CORRECTION

When I train people in the prophetic, I don't allow them to bring correction with a prophetic word. I believe that if you see something corrective, that needs to be taken to leadership and pastors. We pastor people through things, we don't want to expose or shame them. We want to love people back to health.

If I see that someone is moving in the wrong direction, I can speak to them or their leadership, but I'm not going to expose them in front of others. That's an old paradigm of the prophetic, and one that caused a lot of pain for people which was unnecessary. That's not about encouragement or edification or comfort. Pastors will walk people through their healing. God can reveal issues through the prophetic words, and they need to be loved back to health within their own community and their leadership.

When we prophesy, we can sometimes see people at their least loveable—but when they need loved the most. If you see people in the middle of a hard time, just love them well. Always ask God: "How do you see them?"

MOVE IN AUTHORITY & LOVE

Authority is when you have accountability and responsibility. God doesn't take over your body when you prophesy: you are responsible for how you deliver a word. Wrap everything you do in love. Our job is to build a friendship first and foremost. Our job is to declare life and hope. Our job is to call the dry bones to life.

Our church has had events called Destiny Nights. We gather all our prophetic teams. People bring family and friends, and we prophesy over them. The first time we did this, sixty people signed up for a prophetic word. At the end of the night, a man came up and said, "That was so good. I just needed Jesus with skin on tonight." Yes! We want to be Jesus with skin on. We want to represent Him really well. I hope that addressing these protocols and pitfalls will help you represent Him really well.

THE HEART OF PROPHECY

For who knows a person's thoughts except their own spirit within them? In the same way no one knows the thoughts of God except the Spirit of God.

—CORINTHIANS 2:11 NIV

Who can know the heart of God except the Spirit of God? We want to build a friendship with the Spirit of God. Through that friendship, we will learn the mind and heart of God.

Revelation comes from His spirit connecting with our spirit. It's not through our mind—though we can and do use our minds. Revelation comes through the spirit, so we want to sensitize our spirit to Holy Spirit.

When I was young, the church I attended talked about the Father and Jesus, but not much talk about Holy Spirit. In fact, Holy Spirit was sometimes referred to as "it." He was pretty much ignored. I wondered if it was even OK to pray to the Holy Spirit! It's important to realize that Holy Spirit is a person, and we can build a friendship with Him. He's beautiful, and He will reveal Jesus. When you have a friendship with Holy Spirit, you'll get to know the rest of the Godhead even more.

HOW DOES HOLY SPIRIT GET YOUR ATTENTION?

As we sensitize ourselves to the Holy Spirit, we learn new ways of hearing Him. When some people receive words of knowledge, especially around healing, they will start to feel things in their body. Our spirit will affect our body; we are interwoven, body, soul, and spirit. Pay attention to how Holy Spirit talks. If you have a sudden pain in your knee, maybe someone needs healing in their knee; Holy Spirit may be pointing out where the healing needs to happen.

I love prophetic song. Sometimes, when I'm in worship, I'll start to feel a burning in my chest, and I quickly learned that Holy Spirit was telling me He wanted to move in prophetic song.

Pay attention to how Holy Spirit ignites your spirit. What do you feel when He's moving? Mark those feelings.

OUR JOB IS TO GROW IN AWARENESS

Remember: our problem isn't proximity—it's not about distance from God. The problem is our awareness that God is right with us. And we're not always aware of who we are and whose we are. If we can build our awareness in those things, it will change everything.

How do we grow in this friendship? We don't get an impartation of friendship. Like any friendship, we build it step by step with the person. We don't just want head knowledge of Holy Spirit. It's good to know Scripture of course, but we have to experience who He his.

I'd like to share a few ways that I, personally, have built a friendship with the Holy Spirit. I've done so through:

1. **Worship**

2. **Adoration**

3. **Meditation**

4. **Listening to and reading Scripture:** the *logos*, the word of God, is alive and active. You can interact with live things. Think of John 3:16: if you're a Christian, you've already interacted with that word. You've probably also experienced the fruit of the Holy Spirit: love, joy, peace— all of those things.

5. **My imagination:** I'd like to explore this one for a bit…

THE IMAGINATION

Sometimes we're afraid to talk about the imagination, but I want to give you a scriptural context for imagination; it has completely changed my worship and prayer life.

In Ephesians 1:18, Paul prays that "the eyes of your heart may be enlightened, so that you will know what is the hope of His calling, what are the riches of the glory of His inheritance in the saints" (NASB). The word *heart* here is sometimes translated as *understanding*, and in The Passion Translation, it's translated as "the eyes of your imagination." And the purpose? To experience the full revelation of the hope that we are called to.

If the eyes of our imagination are not open, does that mean we don't see a full revelation of what we've been called to? Imagination is what God uses to speak to you. It's how we see in the spirit. Your imagination is actually neutral; it's not bad, and it's not good. It's what we *feed* our imagination that is bad or good.

Think of your imagination as a movie screen. Whatever you feed into the movie projector is what will be projected on that screen.

Say you're a parent, and you're thinking about your child, and fear drops into your spirit. You feel the fear. Then you start to imagine your child being abducted or run over by a bus; you start to play this out in your imagination until you're so stressed and anxious that you begin to build a reality from a fear. That's you building in the spirit. What do you want to build?

Say you're in church, and a friend comes to you and says, "I thought I felt a strong presence of God come into the room," or "I thought I saw an angel." Or say you're in prayer at home worshiping and a thought drops into your spirit. We tend to say: "that's just my imagination." But we don't do that with fear and doubt and worry—we run with those negative things. Let's run with the things God is saying, instead!

Imagine when Samuel was lying in bed as a young boy and hear someone calling him. He rose and went to Eli and said, "Did you call me?" This happened again. And again. The third time, Eli told him: "The next time you hear the voice, say, 'Father, I can hear you. What is it you're speaking to me.'"

If Eli had said to Samuel, , "It's just your imagination." what would the consequences have been?

We often train this hearing out of ourselves and out of our children. We dismiss things by thinking it's just us making stuff up.

I've had friends whose children had imaginary friends. Because we don't know what to do with that, we tend to train it out of them. But these children are using their imagination, and God can use that to build a friendship with them.

The Rabbis would say what we build in the spirit will become our reality. The imaginary realm is a real realm. If you are reading this in a room, that room was first built in the imagination. The floor plan, electricity, lights, furniture—all of it was first built in the imagination.

Steve Jobs wrote about seeing a personal computer in his imagination—before it was a "reality." What we build in our imagination will become our reality. What if we started to say, "It's my imagination" in a good, celebratory sense—not a dismissive one?

What if we built from Heaven's perspective? That's why Philippians 4:8 instructs us to think on true, noble, right and pure things; what we think about we project onto our imagination. Whatever we think about, meditate on, and consider, we project onto the screen of our imagination. Let's do that with Heaven.

That's one of the wonderful things about the prophetic; we train ourselves to see from Heaven's perspective. We should be the most peaceful, joyful, and hopeful people. If we're not, we need to retrain ourselves to think from Heaven's perspective.

WE CAN CULTIVATE THE SENSES OF OUR SPIRIT

We live in a Western world that must see, taste, touch, smell, and feel a thing for it to exist. As Christians, we know there is a real spirit realm beyond our natural senses.

We are body, soul, and spirit. Each of those elements has five senses. I want to challenge you to think about your spirit having each of those five senses. In Ezekiel 3, God came to Ezekiel in a vision and told him to take the scroll and eat it. In the spirit, Ezekiel ate the scroll and said it tasted sweet. That wasn't a physical taste; he tasted with his spirit.

You can hear in the spirit. In corporate worship, we have heard angels singing with our spirit.

In the Book of Revelation, John saw the Lamb and the incense...I'm sure he could see, and hear, and smell that.

Why is it important to cultivate our spirit senses? We can tend to wait for something external to happen to us when we already have access to the Spirit. Of course, great external things can and do happen, but it's important to grow our awareness of Heaven.

I remember as young Christian, prayer was hard for me. "Prayer can start as a work, but it moves into a place of joy."- Clark Taylor. I believe it does so when it becomes interactive experience—not just head knowledge.

If you are my friend, I don't just want to read things about you, I want to experience you. I want to learn what you like, to hear you laugh, to know what moves you. It's the same with the Holy Spirit; we want to build a real, interactive friendship with Him.

WHAT DO WE ALREADY KNOW?

- We know that Satan has been defeated at the Cross.

- We know God is a good Father.

- We know we are children of God.

- We know that the Holy Spirit lives in us.

- We know the authority we walk in will destroy the works of the devil.

In Psalm 46:10 we read: "Be still, and know that I am God" (NIV). The Greek word *yada*—translated here as *know*—is not intellectual knowing. It's experiential knowing. It's about knowing—experiencing—God with all of your senses. When you spend time with God, when you imagine and experience those truths, you can withstand the giants that come against you. They aren't bigger than Jesus.

Sometimes we think doubt is a form of wisdom. No: Doubt is our enemy. We are to be people of faith, believing that God is who He says He is.

If you'd like to increase the good stuff (like faith) and decrease the bad stuff (like doubt), try these exercises during your prayer time:

1. **For getting rid of a negative thought or feeling:** Take doubt, for example. Close your eyes, "see" doubt—visualize it. Now imagine yourself throwing it away. You can do that again and again. That's using your imagination to deal with things in the spirit.

2. **For moving from your head to your heart:** Clark Taylor suggests imagining yourself looking at an elevator. You get into the elevator, and you ride the elevator from your head down to your heart, the spirit. When you imagine the door opening, you've entered the spirit. Imagine yourself with God there. Look around the landscape, go spend time with God there. This is a tool, but if you prac-

tice enough, you don't need to imagine the elevator you can be in that place with God in seconds. I encourage people to practice this in worship, as I find that one of the easiest places to do that. As the doors open each time, a new scene appears, and God has always something he wants to say to us.

3. **For training your spirit senses:** Think of Psalm 23. Begin to imagine those lines. Start seeing those green pastures, smelling the green pastures. What does it feel like on your skin to lie down in green pastures? Taking time to do this is really important, it becomes interactive spending time with God and meditating on His word.

4. **For feeling God's presence:** Sometimes, we can't feel God's presence, even when we try these sorts of exercises. Try asking yourself this: "What if I *could* feel God's presence? Use your imagination! You would probably feel peaceful, secure, confident. As you think about those words, begin to consciously feel and experience them. Those feelings are real, and you're building that reality in the spirit realm with God.

What we think about, we feel, and we release. It works with good and bad things; just like I mentioned before, we are so practiced in the negative thoughts with our imagination, we imagine it until we can feel it, especially fear, and then we release that to the people around us. Let's focus on the things we want to see more of.

When I'm in prayer and say the name *Jesus*, I begin to experience Him because I've experienced His presence, and I've trained my awareness to His presence.

Prayer is not about waiting for something to happen to you. As Shane Willard says, it's not calling on God to come to us, it's about stepping into the flow that is already present.

There are no limits to ways we can encounter and experience God—only the limits we put on ourselves. God is limitless. Our experience of Him is limitless, too. Let this relationship go farther than you can possibly imagine.

Father, I pray that whoever is reading this will develop a place of prayer that will become alive to them. I pray that as they practice your presence they would grow in understanding of who you are and how good you really are. And may this experience affect every area of their life. In Jesus' name, Amen.

ACTIVATIONS

STIRRING UP THE GIFT

As you grow in hearing God's voice, I'd like to pass on a few helpful things I've learned.

Sometimes, we can become passive and just expect God to drop a prophetic word into our spirit. God can certainly do that; He can bring us things in dream, give us thoughts, Scriptures, pictures.

But Paul told Timothy to stir up the gifts within him. There are times when you'll have an opportunity to give someone prophetic word, but you feel like you haven't nothing to give. Remember: it's not about *you* giving a prophetic word. It's about what Holy Spirit is saying and what *He* wants to convey. Sometimes the best way to active our hearing is by encouraging.

The first automobiles had to be cranked to get the engine going. That's like stirring the prophetic well within us. If we are trying to prophecy, we can start stirring up that well by encouraging and blessing. For example, if I'm standing in front of someone, and I don't have a specific word for them, I will start by saying, "Father, I bless Mary. I thank you for her, for the woman she is. I thank you that she is hungry for you."

That starts a flow, and God will start to give me pictures, a sense of His heart for them—all kinds of things. Then I can continue prophesying.

That's why we do activations; we want to stir up the gift. And we can start prophecy from encouragement, letting it lead into a prophetic word.

Prophetic words don't always come quickly as nice packages—though they can. But we can always stir up the prophetic.

TRAINING YOUR SENSES

In Jeremiah 1:11, the Lord asks Jeremiah a question that is important for us to keep in mind. The Lord asks him: What do you see? And Jeremiah describes an almond tree. The Lord asks again: What do you see? And Jeremiah continues to tell the Lord what he sees.

As prophetic people who want to sensitize our spirits, I think it's important to ask the question of ourselves: What do I see? What do I see the Father doing?

When you meet people, ask the Father to see what He is doing. Ask how you can partner with Him.

We have a fun activation to practice this. We partner up with people and look for an article of clothing they're wearing that stands out. Say a red shirt or beautiful shoes. And we use that piece as a springboard to start prophesying. Something like, "I noticed your red shoes, and I immediately felt like the Lord was saying…"

This is a fun way to train your senses to practicing seeing and to quickly catch what God is doing. If you're in a restaurant, and you'd like to encourage your server, you have maybe a minute. This exercise can help you practice a quick response.

I encourage you to find people you can practice with. Get into pairs and start prophesying over each other using a visual springboard. What we see in the natural can open into the supernatural

A SAMPLE ACTIVATION

One of the best ways to practice hearing God's voice is through activations. We have an activation based on Psalm 23 that is especially helpful when you're learning.

Get into groups or 3 or 4. Read through Psalm 23, and then ask Holy Spirit what He'd like to say to the person to your right.

Often, one of the verses in the Psalm will jump out at you, and it will be entirely relevant for the person. This is a great activation, because you can't really go wrong with Scripture. It's a safe way to ask God what He has to say.

And after you've shared that verse, you can ask, "Lord, is there more you have for this person?" Say the part about God leading you beside still waters jumps out at you for the person on your right. You can ask if there's anything else about that passage for the person. God loves encouraging us. He loves comforting us. He loves strengthening us. And He loves doing all of this with us.

Give it a try! See what the fruit is.

MORE ACTIVATIONS TO GET YOU STARTED

1. Ask someone in a group to stand up. Have everyone speak a word that comes to mind for that person.

2. Get into small groups. Start with one person and ask God to give you something for them—a picture, Scripture, impression. Do the same for everyone in the group.

3. Arrange people in two lines, facing each other. Everyone gives the person across from them a word.

4. Make two circles of people: one circle on the outside and one on the inside. Everyone tells the person facing them, "When I look at you, I see..." and then rotate the circles.

5. Have everyone write their name on a piece of paper and fold the paper in half. Everyone passes around the names and takes one or draws one from a hat. Keeping the paper folded, ask God for a prophetic word for the person whose name is on the paper and then give it to them.

6. Sit three people in chairs at the front of the room. Everyone else forms a line in front of them and gives prophetic words as they approach.

7. Gather three people at the front of the room: one prophesies, one asks questions, and one receives. Rotate.

8. Walk around a room and touch people on the head. As you do, ask for the rest of the room to give that person a prophetic word.

9. Choose someone and have the rest of the group ask for a word of knowledge for that person. Get feedback and see how accurate the words are.

ALL YOUR QUESTIONS ANSWERED

In the this chapter I interviewed a variety of people I know, those who are moving in the prophetic and are still on their journey. I always find it helpful to hear how others got to be where they are, what difficulties did they encounter and what where their turning points that helped them progress. I hope you enjoy these different interviews, and find answers for any questions you might have. While all our journeys are different, there are some commonalities that we all share. I pray you find encouragement and continue on your own journey hearing the voice of love, because it is the most important voice in our lives.

IAN AND RACHEL ON PROPHETIC CULTURE

Rachel: I'd like to share what it has looked like for us to build a prophetic culture. For leaders, it can be a little scary. We'd love to share our hearts and experiences with you.

Ian: I think we've made enough mistakes for everybody. We can share our mistakes and some of the glorious things that have happened. We didn't have a prophetic culture. At times, we had the operation of prophecy happening, but certainly not the culture. When I encountered Bethel Church in Redding, I thought it was a special place and wondered what was so special about it. I started reading and listening to their materials. I realized that our values probably needed to shift. We wanted to have a culture of honor, but we didn't know how to create one. So we started a journey of learning.

The prophetic culture is one of the veins of gold that runs through healthy church culture because it affects absolutely everything. And fundamental to it is the notion of calling out the gold in others. It can be wonderful to be in a culture with long-term history and relationship, but one of the downfalls can be that you end up defining each other by the flesh and not the spirit. The prophetic culture helps you to define people by the spirit—not by their mistakes, not by your history but by their call and destiny.

Rachel: When people enter a church with a prophetic culture, they can sense it and experience it. It's obvious when a church has been trained to call out the gold in others; it's a culture of encouragement, of always seeing from Heaven's perspective. I think that being in a place of safety and encouragement will change people the most. We grow through encouragement.

Ian: This word "culture" is everywhere right now. The business world is all about changing company culture—it's culture this and culture that: culture of honor, culture of Sonship, culture of generosity. So what exactly is a culture? For me, it's the atmosphere. It's like when Saul was anointed and met a company of prophets; he began prophesying because he entered their atmosphere, their culture. That atmosphere is largely created by shared values and language.

But not all values are heavenly values. Some are political or religious. Some are handed down to us. We need to examine our values and align them with Heaven. We started looking around at churches and asking, "What are their values? And how do I need to change to embrace that value?"

Rachel: I think sometimes as leaders you think you have certain values in place...until you realize you don't. In building this prophetic culture, it's important to know your values. Everything flows from the top down: from the leader to the congregation. If you're not practicing and speaking into your values, they won't be established, and you won't be able to build a strong foundation needed for a healthy prophetic culture.

Ian: Yes. I don't think you'll create a culture around you that you don't have inside you. For me that means you learn everything you can about the culture and values you want to build. I'm a fan of Danny Silk, so I read his books, listen to his teachings, I go to his events; I make the sacrifice and commitment to do that. If you're going after T.D. Jakes' culture, go after it with everything.

And truthfully, you won't know your values until conflict arises. Rachel and I have been married for a long time. At our wedding, I saw Rachel come down the aisle, I thought, "This is fantastic. Our life starts right here." We had never had an argument.

Rachel: We thought we were so different from everyone else!

Ian: We thought we were too much in love to argue. We didn't actually know what marriage was until conflict was introduced. I would suggest you don't know your values until they meet with conflict. Don't be afraid of conflict. You won't create around you what's not inside you.

Rachel: Yes, I think it's about getting as much help as you can—especially if you're starting from scratch and want to build this culture. You need a real hunger. It costs to have a prophetic culture because you have to build so many values that you may not have at this minute. And as you build those values, you will experience conflict because people don't always like change.

Ian: God is in the business of transformation. We're supposed to become more and more like Him. And my guess is: if we're becoming like Him, He isn't changing—we are.

We love the encouraging culture of the prophetic. It's totally worth paying the price for. There will be certain markers in your journey. We're at the place where we're raising up prophets. Can you have a prophetic culture without a prophet? I would say no. But as you move toward having one, you'll likely hit resistance, because people can be afraid of change. If you don't have a prophet in your church, connect with one outside your church. We had a couple of prophets who spoke into our church and helped shape our prophetic culture.

One thing to be careful of: in a prophetic culture, you can actually create overconfident leaders who believe that they are the next Bill Johnson and they don't think they need to learn anything. We work hard to cultivate a culture of Sonship to counter this. I have a t-shirt that says, "Don't be a wee bastard." It's actually a inspired by the King James Version of Hebrews 12:8, "But if ye be without chastisement, whereof all are partakers, then are ye bastards, and not sons." Basically: If you can't take correction, you're a bastard. We try to promote a culture that says: I might be wrong.

Rachel: It's frightening when prophetic people or prophets come to the church but won't receive any feedback, won't be adjusted. Those people, in Danny Silk's words, are scary. We want people who are willing to be corrected and adjusted—people who are willing to have people speak into their lives. If they aren't willing, that's a sign that they aren't a son or daughter.

Ian: I think the issue of Sonship is essentially an issue of sub-mission. But there's been so much abuse of that word in the Church, that it can be hard to hear it. We've been give bad examples of submission. Submission is simply recognizing who has the authority in any environment. If you are the President of the United States of America or the Queen of England, and you enter my home and tell me how to raise my kids, I will say no. My wife and I have the authority to raise our kids.

The issue of submission within the prophetic is about who is in charge. Unfortunately, it can be easy to think that if you hear from God, you have authority. So it's important to train people in your culture to recognize who has the authority.

Twenty years ago, when the prophetic movement started gaining momentum, we would get that one hurt person in our church who would stand up in the church and say, "Thus sayeth the Lord! You are an abomination in the eyes of Jesus and He's coming to destroy you!" Church leaders didn't know how to deal with this. They loved Jesus, and if that was truly Jesus speaking, they didn't want to ignore Him. As a result of such "prophecies," many people closed down the prophetic. I think we're in a healthier place now. We don't just want to raise up apostles and prophets; we want to raise up healthy apostles and prophets.

That said, I think the journey of creating a prophetic culture is worth it. Creating Heaven's culture on earth makes it a lot easier for Heaven to invade earth.

And while we believe that the Kingdom has come, we also believe the Kingdom is advancing. We want to see more of the Kingdom—not less. Creating this culture is one of the best ways we have found to do that.

But it's a process. Don't be afraid. Learn from the people with values you want to cultivate. And don't just do that remotely; try to find someone who can be involved in your life and ministry.

Rachel: A prophetic culture will effect everything in your church: the worship, the kids' ministry, how you pray for healing, how you minister on Sunday morning. It will bleed into everything in a great way. It makes a place for Heaven to land. Heaven is attracted to prophetic culture because prophetic culture creates awareness of Heaven.

Ian: One last thing: your prophetic ministry will need to be pastored, so your pastors need to be involved in this culture. As the prophetic grace increases, so does the need for the other five-fold graces.

INTERVIEWS

INTERVIEW 1: LACIE

Lacie has been part of my prophetic team for years as well as being part of my leadership team. Here are some questions that I asked Lacie, and I hope as a result will encourage you as you grow in hearing God's voice.

Rachel:. what has your journey in hearing God's voice been like? And when you're prophesying, what does that look like for you?

Lacie: My journey has been very slow because I had to first learn to hear His voice, to trust Him and to trust Holy Spirit—and [to believe] that I have the ability to hear and receive and give out. My journey has been so nonstop since I've been here with Rachel. So now when the Holy Spirit speaks to me, He highlights a person, and I go to that person—with courage and risk—and He gives me a word. All I do is say that word. And guess what? Everything else flows. And I trust. I've learned to trust what Holy Spirit says.

.

Rachel: Are there any times you hear something and know it's not the Holy Spirit? How do you discern when He speaks to you?

Lacie: I feel love, I feel compassion when He speaks to me. Even if I see junk, I press in and ask to see what God sees. He'll start showing me the gold of people, and I can release that. It comes from an intimate feeling of peace with God.

Rachel: Would you say God is a trustworthy to come when you prophesy?

Lacie: When I see people shift from fear to laughter, from tears to smiles—it's a like a resurrection in people. You know it's God because you see the transformation in people.

Rachel: Thank you, Lacie!

INTERVIEW 2: JAMIE GALLOWAY

I'd like to introduce you to everyone to my dear friend Jamie Galloway. I met Jamie when we did a conference together and had the best time. It was really fun, wasn't it?

Jamie: It was a blast. You guys always put on the best events.

Rachel:. This book is about growing in the prophetic, and it's about the basic foundation stuff. Can I ask you a few questions about your own journey?

Jamie: Yes, absolutely.

Rachel: How did you get started on your journey?

Jamie: I grew up knowing the Lord, but the prophetic journey I'm on now began in the atmosphere where I grew up, in St. Louis, Missouri, that made me hunger for the prophetic. There were a lot of prophetic conferences and people, and I was intrigued. When I got around these people, I felt more pathetic than prophetic. I was so blown away by how accurate they were. It frustrated me. So I started trying to prophesy myself, and after many failures, I almost gave up.

Someone came to a meeting I was attending. This guy called me out and said: "God is going to give you a gift, and you're going to prophesy." It didn't immediately happen. It was about nine months after that when I was out at Rainbow Gatherings—pagan festivals. I was ministering in this gathering of 50,000 hippies, gutter punks, witches and warlocks in the middle of the woods, and this Indian prophet showed up wearing his garb. He had planted over 160 churches, but he felt like he was supposed to come to this event. I shadowed him for the entire day, and at the end, I "caught" whatever it was that was on him, and I began to prophesy. It just clicked.

Rachel: We talk about taking our gift to the gym and doing the reps. You obviously didn't start off fully prophesying. And I've heard you prophesy; you've prophesied over Ian and I, and it's very powerful—some of the most prophetic words we've received. But would you say that it was a journey to get to that point?

Jamie: Yes. I had to steward this. It's like we get a spark, but our responsibility is to turn that spark into a bonfire. I received the spark, but I had to nurture it. There was a point about four or five years ago that I determined to take what I was given to the next level. At every event I did, I prophesied for an hour or an hour and a half for each session. I would call people out all day. As I did that, I learned things. It's like logging your hours. At one point, things began to shift.

You have to stay sharp because you can get rusty. Sometimes it takes me a couple of days to get back into the flow if I've been out of practice.

Rachel: We can think that God has given us a gift, and it will just magically unfold, but that's not how it works. As you say, you have to keep practicing, and at some point there will be breakthrough.

Jamie: Absolutely.

Rachel: How would you say God speaks to you personally?

Jamie: I [mostly] hear God through impressions and what I call seer moments—those could be a vision, a dream, or something in real life that catches my eye, and I want to find out more. The impressions are like inner visions. It's like being in a daydream you didn't know was happening until it's done. For me personally, it's the still small voice. I'm just listening, and I'm paying attention. That was the original way I started hearing the voice of God.

I distinguish between hearing God's voice and recognizing the message. We could hear his voice through an angel, a messenger prophet—but we have to recognize the message. Even with the prophet Elijah—he heard thunder, lightening, and he had to learn to hear the voice of God.

Rachel: So has that been a growth process as well?

Jamie: Yes. All of it has been a process that the Holy Spirit has taken me through. When we're faithful with the measure we've been given, we'll begin to see increase. Sometimes you hit a moment when multiplication happens. Those times are always fun. I've had some out-there encounters—out-of-body experiences, being taken to heaven—all of that stuff. If I steward the still small voice in my life, those things happen more frequently.

Rachel: What would you say to the people who are just starting to grow in the prophetic? Is there one thing you would say is a key to help them?

Jamie: Above everything else, I am such a believer in mentorship and finding the right mentors. A professional athlete has about five coaches. The average individual in the church has one pastor—split between 3,000 people! That's just terrible. How are we going to grow if we don't have mentors—spiritual mothers and fathers? I believe in seeking out those mentors and honoring them.

Rachel, if I come to you for mentorship, I need to know the cost. There needs to be reciprocity. How can I add value to you as you add value to me? How can I bless you while you're blessing me?

A gift makes rooms for you. We tend to think that's spiritual, but a gift can also be an act of service: washing a person's dishes or financing their vision. That gift makes room for you.

My first mentor was a mystical prophet. One thing he needed help with was to make 500 copies a week—brochures and things. So I did that every week for him. It took me an entire day. Because I did that, he made time for me. An easy way to find a mentor is to make yourself useful.

Rachel: I remember when Tiger Woods was one of the top golfers, he still had a coach—who couldn't even play as well as him. But the coach could help Tiger see how to improve. We need to be around people who can helps us, and it's not just a one-way relationship.

I know you travel and speak and have resources—and a course on seers. How can we access those resources?

Jamie: If you go to JamieGalloway.com/secrets, you'll find a free download and audio and more information [on the] Seer Masterclass. I believe that everyone is a seer—we just don't all know what to look for. We need to be trained and coached.

I've been able to interview many people for that class, and I've gleaned from others, so I've put together an amazing course that I believe will increase your ability to see.

Rachel. Fantastic. One last thing. You're someone I've heard the most amazing and weird stories from—do you have an experience you could tell us here?

Jamie: There are so many stories and fun encounters. You collect them along the way and realize how bizarre your life is! Recently, I was at the end of a conference in Iowa, and I saw couple at the front. I could see in the spirit that they were in a legal battle. To me, that looked like they were in a courtroom setting with confusing papers.

At this point, I was exhausted. It was the end of the conference. I actually made an announcement: "I've got one more prophecy in me, and I'm going to give it you. I see you're in a legal battle so bad, you can't even show your face. But God is going to give you favor with the judge. The case will be overturned and ruled in your favor." I saw the pastor walk over from his seat and wrap his arms around the couple.

As I was getting in my car after, the pastor came up to me and said, "Jamie, I thought you were way off. That couple is on my core team. I know everything there is to know about that couple. When I walked over to them, I went to console them about the prophecy you gave them that I thought was a false prophecy! I told them, 'I'm so sorry. Jamie missed it. God's got you.' And they looked at me and said, 'No—you don't understand. We haven't told you...'

Apparently, the man's nephew had made some terrorist threats as a teenager, and the highest level of government had become aware of this and wanted to make a public example of him. The uncle had been going to represent his nephew every week, and the couple couldn't show their faces in town. It was a big deal. They got back to me a couple weeks later. They said that the odds had been totally against them, but the judge ruled in their favor.

God always has a better answer for every situation we're in.

Rachel: The power of the prophetic is that it is something you can hold onto when the circumstances look different. You can stand on God's word.

Thank you so much. You are the real deal. I recommend everyone checks out Jamie's website and resources; they will help you on your journey.

Q & A

We get a lot of questions about the prophetic, so I gathered some of my marvelous team to help answer them. The answers below came from Autumn Starks, Rachel Jumpa, Kristen Henry, and myself....

Q: How do I know that a prophetic word is not just me?

We always go back to Scripture. We always want to measure a word up to Scripture and the character of God. If you do make a mistake, the worst thing you're doing is telling someone something based on Scripture—it's a good safe zone to start in.

If it's encouraging, no one one's going to die. As you begin to prophesy, it's likely to feel 80% you and 20% Holy Spirit. As you grow and gain confidence, that percentage changes.

Get around people who are already prophesying and listen. You'll begin to hear confirmation of things you also heard. God will confirm for you.

It's always better to learn in company; that gives you accountability. When you're training, it's vital to be willing to be adjusted.

God uses everything to speak to us. He can speak through our thoughts—so sometimes, your thoughts can also be his. If you're a strategist, God might speak to you in strategies. If you're a feeler, He will speak to you through your emotions. He wants to partner with you, so there will be a mixture of Him and you.

He speaks your language. He'll use your history with Him to speak to you.

Q. What is one of the main ways I can grow in my prophetic gifting?

Get around people who are practicing. As you take risks, you'll have support and advice.

You can practice with anyone anywhere: on Facebook, via text message, with the barista at Starbucks. Just practice. Ask the Father for a word every day and give that word. And it will get addictive as you see God's heart for people and you see them encouraged.

Build up your history with God; practice your reps. Push yourself out of your comfort zone—we can't grow if we stay comfortable.

And ask people for feedback: "Did that make sense?" Ask God questions.

Q: What do I do if I start moving in the prophetic, but the church I go to doesn't believe in the gifts?

It's difficult to grow in a place where something isn't nurtured—no matter what it is. I don't know how you grow in soil that doesn't have the nutrients you need. That might be a hard conversation you have with yourself: "Is this the best place for me?" In churches, the anointing flows from the leadership down. If you're in a church and you think: "I'm going to change my leaders," that's unhealthy and manipulative. This is a difficult question, because leaders set the culture, and you want to honor them—but you're likely to be stunted in your growth.

Cultivate what you have and what you can. If your church isn't recognizing your gift, follow Holy Spirit's leading. He always wants to let His love be known.

Ask permission. Tell someone that you hear something encouraging from the Lord for them, can you share it?

Sometimes, pastors are afraid of the lone-ranger prophet walking into their church and thinking they can tell them what to do. That's not what the prophetic is about. But if you do have a relationship with your pastor and you tell them about what you're learning, and how encouraging it is, they might be more receptive. Don't be scary to your leaders. It's always about serving and encouraging.

The Holy Spirit who gives you a word for someone is the same Holy Spirit who will give you guidance on how to approach them—leadership included.

And if you're at the place to ask this question, you probably need a mentor who has walked people through these conversations before.

Prophetic people can be really sensitive, so if you feel isolated or hurt by your leaders, you need someone who can come alongside you and walk you through. If it gets to the point that you feel you need to leave your church, ask God for someone to encourage you.

Q: What do I do if I've been receiving revelation but I find myself in a season when it's hard to hear from the Lord?
Pray!

Just like with anything in life, things changes. A daily relationship with Him will cultivate your hearing and communication so that on those days when it's harder to hear, you know to press in and spend a more time in His presence.

Keep taking risks.

I think He's in the process of training us, and if we get too comfortable hearing Him in just one way, He might stir up a level of hunger in you. Reframe the idea that God is abandoning you into the idea that God is allowing you to become more hungry for Him. Keep your eyes and ears and heart open to new ways He's drawing us to Him. The Holy Spirit is a counselor, and counselors help us see our blind spots.

If you feel that God isn't speaking to you, you are probably believing something about God that isn't true. Those times are hard, but press into God's nature.

Don't panic and don't strive to hear His voice. It's the voice of Love. There are times you're holding fast, and there are times you're being held. That's when you call on your community and admit that you're struggling.

When I feel like I can't hear God, I always go back to the last thing He said. Go back to worship. Go back to where you began with Him. God had the Israelites build memorials for remembrance. Revisit your own testimonies.

Q: I know from Scripture that everyone can prophesy, but does everyone have the gift of prophecy?
The Bible does say that we all can prophesy, but I would say that we don't all have the gift of prophecy. What is the

difference? We can all prophesy. Just entering a prophetic atmosphere can ignite the prophetic in you, and you can begin to prophesy. The gift of prophecy is a gift of the Holy Spirit, and I believe it's something that you have been given—it's been developed in you even before you might have recognized it.

I Corinthians 14 tells us that we can all prophesy to encourage and build up, but I think that having the gift of prophecy is all of the things under the umbrella of prophecy and having a hunger for those things. Someone with the gift of prophecy has a deep hunger for it. When you're around prophets, you want more.

If, as you read this, you feel a hunger stirred up, you might have the gift of prophecy.

We're all sons and daughters of God. We can all hear His voice. Whether or not you have the gift of prophecy, you can hear the voice of God. The gift just takes it up a level and helps you share that voice with others.

Q: I've begun to operate in prophecy, in receiving revelation, and have started to share the heart of God with others. How do I know if I'm a prophetic person or if I'm called to be a prophet?
I would say that a prophet has a higher level of authority. As a prophet, you are the gift. You can go beyond encouraging people to shifting things with your prophetic words.

According to the five-fold graces in Ephesians 4, one of the main tasks of the prophet is to train and equip and mature the Church Body.

Prophets often train with other prophets who help them grow in their role—and that can accelerate the process.

I would say that the prophet's main job is to move in authority and adjust the Body to bring transformation. There is often a justice and mercy drive in the prophet.

When you're a prophet, you can't think of doing anything else. You live it. You breathe it. You can't stop thinking about God and the call on your life. It's a daily weight.

I think you can be a gifted prophetic person with a call and a destiny to something different than Church adjustment. But prophets are for adjusting the Church.

Jesus calls you to be a prophet. We don't decide to. Along our journey, others recognize the gift you are. You are the gift.

We might think that being a prophet will open doors for us, but it's more of a pure and restricting path. There's a cost that comes with that grace unleashed in your life.

Stay close to Him. If you do, you won't get distracted or try to become something you're not. As long as you stay close to Him, you won't miss anything.

If love is your foundation, you can't go wrong.

ABOUT THE AUTHOR

Rachel Carroll has pursued the prophetic for over twenty Five years. She operates as a prophet and has spent the last few years developing other prophets around her. She is passionate that everyone hears the Fathers voice— because she has seen in her own life, again and again, that the voice of love changes everything.

I hope that you will use this book to come back to again and again. I pray you will use it as a way to help you to lay down a strong foundation for yourself, and to grow in hearing the "Voice of Love." This is a life time journey, you never arrive, you just keep growing and you have no idea where God will take you, or even how He will use you. My best words of wisdom to you is to stay hungry! Feed yourself, again and again, never get complacent. Learn to know His voice as you would your closest friend and it will surprise you what your journey with Him will look like. He loves you so much, and we need you to be all that God has already said you are! The world is waiting for you.